Malaysia

Malaysia

BY MICHAEL BURGAN

Enchantment of the World™
Second Series

CHILDREN'S PRESS®

An Imprint of Scholastic Inc.

Frontispiece: **Paddling to stilt houses**

Consultant: Barbara Watson Andaya, Chair, Asian Studies Program, University of Hawaii at Manoa
Please note: All statistics are as up-to-date as possible at the time of publication.

Book production by The Design Lab

Library of Congress Cataloging-in-Publication Data
Burgan, Michael.
  Malaysia : enchantment of the world / by Michael Burgan.
      pages cm. — (Enchantment of the world)
  Includes bibliographical references and index.
  Audience: Grades 4–6.
  ISBN 978-0-531-21699-6 (library binding)
1. Malaysia—Juvenile literature. I. Title.
  DS592.B87 2015
  959.5—dc23   2014048690

1 2 3 4 5 6 7 8 9 10 R 25 24 23 22 21 20 19 18 17 16

Iban man, Sarawak

Contents

Left to right: **Ipoh, indigenous ritual, beach, Taman Negara National Park, praying at a mosque**

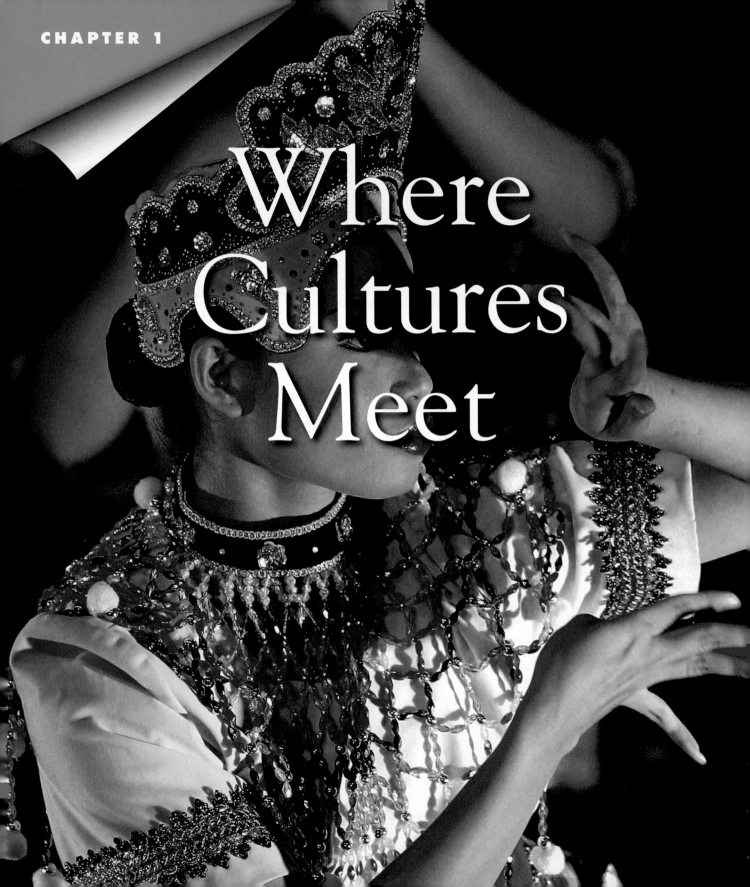

CHAPTER 1

Where Cultures Meet

IN THE SOUTHEAST CORNER OF ASIA, A LONG, NARROW strip of land juts south into the ocean. The nearby waters are filled with many islands. Sea travel and trade have been a way of life in this region for centuries. They have brought people from all over Asia and beyond to what is now the nation of Malaysia. Malaysia covers the tip of that long piece of land, which is called the Malay Peninsula, and part of the large island of Borneo.

Old and New

The country of Malaysia, home to people of many ethnic backgrounds and faiths, is a mix of old and new. In remote parts of the country, far from the cities and the coasts, old ways of life still exist. There, some people hunt, gather wild crops, and live in traditional homes. Traditional rice farming

and fishing have largely disappeared, however, as the country grows wealthier and the government pushes for more modern ways of life throughout Malaysia.

Malaysia's modernity can be seen in the sleek Petronas Towers, the world's tallest twin towers, and other skyscrapers that mark the skyline of Kuala Lumpur, the country's capital.

Crossroads of Southeast Asia

In the past, ships carrying trade between India and China stopped at Malay ports to trade for tin, spices, and other resources. The narrow Strait of Malacca, separating the Malay Peninsula from the nearby island of Sumatra, was a major traffic route. Starting in the sixteenth century, Europeans traded in the region as well. They valued Malaysia's location close to the major Asian nations and the spice-growing islands of the region. Great Britain was the

The Petronas Towers rise 1,483 feet (452 meters) above the ground. That's more than a quarter of a mile.

foreign nation that played the largest role here. It colonized what is now Malaysia, exploiting its resources.

Malaysia had received immigrants from other parts of Asia for several thousands of years before the British arrived. But it was under British rule that large numbers of Chinese and Indians settled alongside the Malay people already there. Together, these three ethnic groups define much of Malaysian culture. But British influences remain, as English is widely spoken, and the British helped Malaysia develop its schools and system of government.

Chinese Malaysians visit a temple in Kuala Lumpur to celebrate Chinese New Year.

Today, Malaysia is a popular spot for tourists, attracting visitors from around the globe. They come for the country's great variety of wildlife, both on land and at sea. They enjoy Malaysia's warm temperatures and beautiful beaches. They taste the famous street food of Penang, with flavors from across Southeast Asia. Visitors and residents alike enjoy this country and its vibrant history, culture, and people.

More than twenty-five million tourists visit Malaysia every year. Many come to relax on the white sand beaches.

Two Regions, One Nation

MALAYSIA IS MADE UP OF TWO SEPARATE landforms separated by a wide swath of water. To the west is Peninsular (or West) Malaysia, which sits on the Malay Peninsula, a long, thin stretch of the Asian mainland. About 400 miles (640 kilometers) across the South China Sea is East Malaysia. East Malaysia covers the northern part of Borneo, the third-largest island in the world. Almost nine hundred smaller islands that lie off the shores of Malaysia's two regions also belong to Malaysia. The largest include Banggi, Langkawi, and Penang. The islands are part of the Malay Archipelago, the largest island group in the world.

West Malaysia is bordered to the north by the country of Thailand. Just off the southern tip of West Malaysia is the

Opposite: **The Langkawi Islands lie off of Peninsular Malaysia.**

Malaysia's Geographic Features

Area: 127,355 square miles (329,848 sq km)

Highest Elevation: Mount Kinabalu, 13,431 feet (4,094 m) above sea level

Lowest Elevation: Sea level, along the coast

Longest Rivers: Rajang and Kinabatangan, each about 350 miles (560 km) long

Largest Island: Borneo (shared with Indonesia and Brunei)

Number of Islands: 878

Average High Temperature: In Kuala Lumpur, 90°F (32°C) in January, 91°F (33°C) in July

Average Low Temperature: In Kuala Lumpur, 74°F (23°C) in January, 75°F (24°C) in July

Average Annual Precipitation: About 150 inches (380 cm) in East Malaysia; 100 inches (250 cm) in West Malaysia

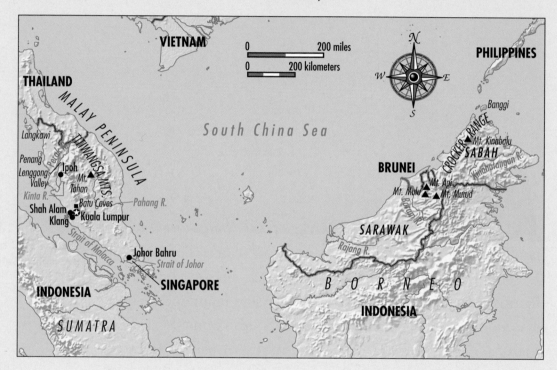

island nation of Singapore and just beyond are large islands in the nation of Indonesia. On Borneo, East Malaysia's southern neighbor is Indonesia. The small nation of Brunei lies on Borneo's northern coast, completely surrounded by East Malaysia.

Exploring West Malaysia

The part of Malaysia that lies on the Malay Peninsula makes up only about one-third of the country's area, but it is home to the vast majority of the country's people. Bordering that coast, separating West Malaysia from the Indonesian island of Sumatra, is a body of water called the Strait of Malacca (sometimes spelled Melaka). This strait connects the Indian Ocean and the Pacific Ocean. In the days of sailing ships, the

The Strait of Malacca runs for about 500 miles (800 km), separating Malaysia (bottom) from the Indonesian island of Sumatra (top).

strait protected vessels from the rough weather out at sea, and it remains one of the busiest waterways in the world.

Along the coastal regions of West Malaysia, the land is flat. Moving inland, hills and mountains run from the Thai border to just south of Kuala Lumpur. The main range is the Titiwangsa Mountains. These steep, rugged mountains are covered with forest and broken by caves. The highest peak on the peninsula is Mount Tahan, at 7,175 feet (2,187 meters). It's located in Taman Negara National Park, east of the capi-

A cable car takes visitors to the top of the Titiwangsa Mountains.

A Cool, Green Place

To escape the frequently hot weather in their Asian colonies, the British founded hill stations. These were towns located at higher elevations, where the temperatures were typically lower than in the coastal regions. The most famous hill station in Malaysia was Cameron Highlands, named for William Cameron. In 1885, he was mapping the countryside for the British government when he found this spot in the center of the Malay Peninsula. He had to cut through thick plant growth to reach it. Sitting at an elevation of between 4,000 and 6,000 feet (1,200 and 1,800 m), the highlands feature beautiful mountain scenery and waterfalls. Cameron didn't mark the location on his maps, and the British did not start a hill station there until decades later. Today, the cool temperatures of the Cameron Highlands offer relief from the heat of other parts of Malaysia.

tal. In the past, the mountains isolated people on one side of the Malay Peninsula from people on the other side. People found it much easier to travel and trade by the sea. As one historian put it, "the land divided and the sea united."

Rain forests and jungles blanket much of the interior of the peninsula, and in the past even more of the land was forested. Many parts of Malaysia are unsuitable for farming because of the country's poor soil. Still, crops are grown in many parts of the country. On the peninsula, these include rubber trees, tea, rice, and oil palm trees.

Several major rivers flow out of the mountains down to the coastal lands. The longest on the peninsula is the Pahang,

A Look at Malaysia's Largest Cities

Most of the major cities of Malaysia are on the Malay Peninsula. After Kuala Lumpur, the capital, which has a population of about 1.6 million, the largest of these is Klang, with a population of about 1.2 million. Klang is about 18 miles (29 km) southwest of Kuala Lumpur. People have been living on the site for more than two thousand years. In the nineteenth century, tin became a major industry in the area around Klang, and the city grew in importance. Today, the city's Tin Museum traces its history and importance to the region. The older section of the city has a former royal palace and a mosque, a Muslim place of worship.

At the southern tip of the peninsula is Johor Bahru (below), which is sometimes called simply JB. This city of just over one million people is the capital of the state of Johor. It sits on one side of the Strait of Johor; Singapore, with which it has strong economic ties, is on the opposite side. While Johor Bahru has some

historic buildings, a popular attraction for young visitors is Legoland Resort Malaysia. Along with rides and a water park, it features models of Asian buildings made out of more than thirty million Lego bricks.

Ipoh (above), north of Kuala Lumpur, has a population of over 700,000. The city, the capital of the state of Perak, was founded in the nineteenth century as tin mining grew in the region. Many Chinese immigrants moved to Ipoh to work in the tin mines. Ipoh is split in half by the Kinta River. On one side is the Old Town, which features many historic buildings, including a grand railway station. Old Town is full of shophouses, which were combined stores and living quarters for Chinese merchants and their families. New Town is the site of the city hall and many stores and hotels.

Much newer than most of Malaysia's cities is Shah Alam, right next to Kuala Lumpur. Shah Alam, which is home to about 671,000 people, was designed to serve as a center of government and commerce and is the capital of the state of Selangor. Its Blue Mosque is the largest mosque in Malaysia.

which runs for about about 300 miles (480 km). The second-longest river is the Perak, at about 250 miles (400 km). Malaysia's first rubber trees were planted along its banks, and its moving water helps power plants generate electricity.

Exploring East Malaysia

Like the Malay Peninsula, the island of Borneo has flat coastal lands and mountainous regions farther in. East Malaysia covers about a quarter of the island.

Thick rain forest covers much of Malaysian Borneo.

Malaysia's tallest peak is Mount Kinabalu, at 13,431 feet (4,094 m). Located in northern Borneo, in the Malaysian state of Sabah, it is part of the Crocker Range, a series of mountains not far from Sabah's western coast. Part of this rugged range is a national forest. It receives up to 158 inches (401 centimeters) of rain each year, and the water is collected and used for farming, industry, and drinking.

To the southwest, in the Malaysian state of Sarawak, lie Mount Mulu and Mount Api, which are part of Gunung Mulu National Park. These mountains boast lush gorges, massive caves, and limestone pinnacles that rise up from the ground like towering daggers.

The Caves of Sarawak

Imagine stepping into a cave wide enough to hold forty jumbo jets at once, or tall enough to fit a building almost 500 feet (150 m) high. Caves this size are found in Gunung Mulu National Park in Sarawak. The park has one of the largest cave systems in the world. Rivers rushing down the mountains long ago carved these caves from the limestone rock. Carbon dioxide, a gas in the air and soil, mixes with the water to form a weak acid. This acid then eats away at the limestone and creates caves. Clearwater Cave, the longest in Asia, still has a river flowing through it. Deer Cave, one of the largest caves in the world, has an entrance so big that enough light enters for trees to grow inside. The cave is also home to almost two million bats. Humans have yet to explore all of the caves' passages.

Sabah and Sarawak each lay claim to Malaysia's longest rivers. The Rajang in Sarawak and the Kinabatangan in Sabah are each about 350 miles (560 km) long. Boats can travel more than 100 miles (160 km) up these rivers, providing access to the interior of the island. Traditionally, people in East Malaysia have lived along the rivers.

Many of the sharp pinnacles in Gunung Mulu National Park rise as high as a fifteen-story building.

A Warm and Wet Land

Across most of Malaysia, the climate is warm, with several rainy seasons during the year. The country sits in the tropics—regions near the equator that typically have high temperatures and humidity. Most of Malaysia sees daily temperatures between 70 and 90 degrees Fahrenheit (21 and 32 degrees Celsius), though in the highlands temperatures can be 10°F (6°C) lower. Clouds

A bicycle cab drives down a street on a rainy day in Penang.

often drift through the sky, even when no rain is falling. But sometimes during the year, when the major winds blow in from the ocean, carrying abundant water with them, the country sees frequent and intense rains. These major wind patterns are called monsoons. Areas close to the coast tend to get the most rainfall, though the west coast of the peninsula is somewhat protected by the nearby mountains.

Malaysia sometimes feels the effects of typhoons, which are major storms that form in the western Pacific Ocean.

(When these storms form off the coasts of North America they are called hurricanes.) Although Malaysia does not usually feel the full force of these storms, the nation sometimes experiences high winds, waves, and rainfall because of them.

At times, heavy rains in a short period can flood streets in coastal cities and towns. In December 2014, the eastern Malay Peninsula experienced the worst flooding in Malaysia in thirty years. More than 160,000 people were forced from their homes as water submerged the streets and poured into houses and businesses.

Floods in December 2014 left entire towns underwater.

CHAPTER 3

Diverse
Life

A HIKER IN THE FORESTS OF MALAYSIA WILL likely see hundreds of different types of flowers. In fact, more than fifteen thousand varieties of flowering trees and plants grow in Malaysia, including several thousand types of orchids alone! Visitors to the mountains or shore will also see a rich variety of animals of all shapes and sizes—from bugs to bats and maybe even bears. Some of the creatures among this wide range of wildlife are endemic to Malaysia, meaning they're found nowhere else on earth.

Opposite: **About 60 percent of the land in Malaysia is covered by forest.**

In the Forest

Much of Malaysia is covered in thick rain forest. The trees in a rain forest form a thick canopy, blocking sunlight from reaching the forest floor. In this dim world beneath the canopy grow

Shrinking Forests

Over the decades, large sections of Malaysia's vast rain forests have been cut down. In some cases, the trees are cut for their timber. But more recently, trees have been cleared so that farmers and large companies could plant crops, particularly oil palm trees. The oil taken from the trees is used in foods and soaps. From 2000 to 2012, Malaysia suffered more deforestation than any other country. When the forests are destroyed, animals lose their habitat. This has endangered various species such as the orangutan and the Malayan tiger. The destruction of forests also makes it harder for people who rely on the forests to get food and the materials they use for tools and clothing. The Malaysian government is trying to find ways to protect the environment while still creating jobs in the palm oil industry.

ferns, vines, and mosses. The rain forests in Borneo are among earth's oldest, dating back about 140 million years. Malaysia also features swampy forests near the coast. Although great swaths of Malaysian forests have been cut in recent years, forests still cover about two-thirds of East Malaysia and more than one-third of West Malaysia.

Flowers and Trees

The forests of Malaysia are home to many kinds of trees—up to six thousand species just in West Malaysia. Trees grown for their lumber include teak and batai. In East Malaysia, Sabah is home to the world's tallest tropical tree, which is also the tallest tree in Asia. This *seraya kuning siput* tree was measured at 292 feet (89 m) in 2006. Another tall forest dweller is the tualang, which is not a tree, but a giant relative of bean and lentil plants. The tualang can grow to heights of about 250 feet (76 m).

The country has many tropical trees that produce edible fruit, such as bananas, mangoes, and papayas. Other fruits that grow in Malaysia are not as well known in North America. For example, Malaysians eat large fruits called durians and sometimes use them to flavor foods such as ice cream, candy, soup, and rice.

Rubber trees are grown on plantations across Malaysia, but they are not native to the country. The British brought them in so they could tap the trees for their sap, called latex, which was turned into rubber.

Across Malaysia, many colorful flowers grow, and the country is famous for its delicate but spectacular orchids. It also has several species of the world's largest flower, the rafflesia. Found mostly in East Malaysia, these flowers

The National Flower

Malaysia's national flower is the Chinese hibiscus. Each bloom of this large red flower has five petals. The red of the flower symbolizes courage and unity. As its name indicates, the flower originated in China. It was likely brought to Malaysia in the twelfth century and is now found throughout the country.

can grow up to 3 feet (1 m) wide. Rafflesias are known for their strong odor, which some people compare to rotting meat. The flower's monstrous bloom lasts only a few days.

The Mammals of Malaysia

While many people think of leopards, rhinoceroses, elephants, and tigers as African animals, all of them can also be found in Malaysia. The Sumatran rhino has two horns and is smaller than its African cousins. The elephants of Malaysia are also smaller than elephants found in Africa.

Malaysia is also home to the orangutan, the only member of the ape family that lives outside of Africa. The orangutan's

Symbol of a Nation

The Malayan tiger is the national animal of Malaysia and appears on the country's coat of arms. It lives in Malaysia's dense forests, where it can easily hide among the thick plant growth. As the animal's habitat has been destroyed, the number of tigers has declined. Today, only a few hundred Malayan tigers survive.

name comes from two Malay words that mean "people of the forest." Orangutans live on Borneo and the Indonesian island of Sumatra. Known for their red fur, these apes are smart enough to make umbrellas out of tree leaves when it rains and use sticks to take honey from beehives.

Orangutans spend most of their time in trees.

Known for Its Nose

Proboscis is another word for nose. Take one look at the proboscis monkey and its obvious how it got its name. The proboscis monkey is found only in the rain forests of Borneo. It spends most of its life in trees, though it sometimes ventures into the water and is an excellent swimmer—the best of all the world's monkeys. Proboscis monkeys sometimes weigh as much as 50 pounds (23 kilograms), making them among the biggest of the monkeys found in Asia. Like many animals of Malaysia, these monkeys are an endangered species because of deforestation.

Diverse Life **31**

Another mammal in Malaysia is a type of tapir. These plant-eating animals are related to rhinoceroces, and the Malayan tapir is the largest of the four types found around the world. They can reach up to 6 feet (1.8 m) long. Malayan tapirs communicate with each other by making a range of whistling sounds. The gaur, a large relative of the cow, is also found in Malaysia. The male gaur has a hump on its shoulders, and both males and females have horns. A male gaur can weigh up to 2,000 pounds (900 kg). The gaur is endangered in Malaysia, with only a few animals remaining.

Malayan tapirs have poor eyesight but an excellent sense of smell.

About three hundred different species of bats can be found in the caves of Malaysia, accounting for about 40 percent of all the mammal species in the country. Bats are important to Malaysian farmers, as they carry pollen and seeds to different places, enabling new plants to grow.

Small bats hang from the roof of a shelter in Malaysia.

Preserving Nature

Malaysia has established many national parks to help preserve its stunning landscapes and the animals that live there. The nation's oldest and largest national park is Taman Negara, which protects a large stretch of rain forest in West Malaysia. Many rare creatures live in the ancient, shadowy forest. Fewer than one hundred Sumatran rhinoceroces still live in Malaysia, but a few survive in Taman Negara. Malayan tigers, Asian elephants, and Malayan tapirs, stout creatures that look something like large pigs, also make the park their home.

The species of frog scientists discovered in Malaysia is so small it can easily sit on the end of a pencil.

Cold-Blooded Creatures

Amphibians and reptiles are cold-blooded. This means they need sunlight to keep their bodies warm and active. Amphibians split their time between land and water, while reptiles live mostly on land. In Malaysia both kinds of wildlife are common across the country.

Malaysia is home to more than two hundred species of amphibians, most of which are frogs and toads. In 2010, scientists working in Malaysia discovered one of the world's smallest frogs. Its official name is *Microhyla nepenthicola*, and it's about the size of a pea! Caecilians are another type of amphibian. These wormlike creatures live only in the tropics. While they don't look threatening, they have many sharp teeth and feed on a variety of animals, including insects and reptiles.

Reptiles found in Malaysia include a wide range of snakes, including cobras and pit vipers. The king cobra is the longest poisonous snake in the world, sometimes reaching lengths of 18 feet (5.5 m). Like many other snakes, it usually tries to avoid conflict. But when threatened, it does sometimes bite, and its poisonous bite can kill an elephant! In the rain forests of the Malay Peninsula, visitors who look up might see paradise tree snakes moving from tree to tree. They're called flying snakes, but they don't actually fly. Instead, they flatten their bodies and glide through the air. They can cover 300 feet (90 m) in a single leap from a high tree to a lower one.

The king cobra primarily preys on other snakes, although it will occasionally eat lizards, birds, and rodents.

Other reptiles in Malaysia are lizards ranging from tiny geckos to large, powerful monitor lizards. Found in Malaysia's coastal waters, the monitor lizards are among the heaviest lizards in the world and can reach up to 6 feet (1.8 m) in length. Also in the country's waters are crocodiles and four species of sea turtles. These include the leatherback and the hawksbill. Like other sea turtles, they come ashore only to lay their eggs.

Colorful Sea Life

Under the waters off Malaysia live some of the world's most diverse coral reefs, with more than 350 different coral species. The reefs might look like unmoving rocks or plants, but the corals are alive, breathing and eating as other creatures do. The reefs are also home to colorful tropical fish, such as clown fish, sea horses, and mandarin fish. Some of these beautiful fish

Saving Sea Turtles

A number of animals—including humans—find sea turtle eggs tasty treats to eat. That's just one reason the number of sea turtles in Malaysia has fallen, with the leatherback sea turtle becoming especially endangered. The country now has a number of sanctuaries, or protected areas, where the sea turtles can come ashore and lay their eggs in safety. This protection also gives the hatched baby turtles time to grow so they'll be strong enough to return to the sea. Visitors to the sanctuaries can watch the turtles come ashore to lay their eggs and see the young turtles swimming in small pools of seawater.

can be deadly. For protection, the lionfish, for example, has spines on its body filled with poison.

One fish commonly found in reefs is the bigeye trevally. It and other trevallies are popular with fishers. All kinds of seafood, including shellfish, squid, crabs, and deepsea fish such as marlins, mackerels, snappers, and groupers, are popular in Malaysian cooking.

The lionfish uses the venom in its spines to ward off attackers. The painful sting can cause breathing difficulties in humans.

On the Wing

High in the trees or soaring through the skies, birds of all kinds live in Malaysia. More than seven hundred species inhabit the country's two regions. Some live in Malaysia year-round, while others are migratory—they pass through Malaysia on their way to other locations.

Swiftlets are common in Malaysia. Many swiftlets live in caves on Borneo, while others live elsewhere in the country. Like bats, cave swiftlets use sound waves to help them find their way in the dark. They do this by emitting sounds that bounce off the cave walls and return back to them. Some swiftlet nests are edible, and are especially popular in China, where they're featured in soups. People who harvest these nests must climb tall ladders to reach them, because the birds build the nests high on the cave walls.

In the rain forests, some birds fly among the tall trees while others walk along the forest floor. The crested argus spends much time in the high branches of the trees. Like a peacock, the crested argus has long tail feathers. The male's tail feathers are among the longest of any bird in the world, sometimes growing to lengths of 6 feet (1.8 m). Another bird frequently found in the forest is the rhinoceros hornbill. This bird gets its name from its casque, a growth on the top of its head that looks something like a rhino's horn.

Malaysia is home to many waterbirds such as egrets and herons. It also supports many birds that hunt other animals. These birds of prey include eagles, hawks, and vultures.

The rhinoceros hornbill plays a significant role in Malaysian culture. Among some groups it is considered the king of birds or a symbol of power.

Going Buggy

Around the world, scientists have identified one million insect species, and thousands of them live in Malaysia. Many types of Malaysian insects, such as beetles, bees, ants, and grasshoppers, are also common in North America.

Malaysia can also claim some very unusual insects. The giant walking stick belongs to the longest insect family on earth and can reach a length of 2 feet (60 cm). As its name suggests, it looks like a stick, which helps it blend in with surrounding tree branches and hide from animals that might want to eat it. The orchid mantis, a type of praying mantis, looks almost just like the orchids it lives on. This camouflage helps the mantis remain hidden while it hunts other insects that come to the flower.

A zookeeper holds a Malaysian giant walking stick. Walking sticks are active mostly at night, when they move around to feed on leaves.

Thousands of butterfly species make their home in Malaysia. These include the Rajah Brooke's birdwing, a large butterfly with vivid green markings. Birdwing butterflies get their name from the shape of their wings, which are pointed and stream-lined like the wings of birds.

Male Rajah Brooke's birdwings are bright green, while females are brown.

Killer Bug

Around the world, there are many kinds of assassin bugs, but one type in Malaysia has a special way of protecting itself. Like other bugs of its kind, the assassin bug kills, or assassinates, its prey by piercing it repeatedly with its pointed proboscis, its long tubelike mouth. The assassin bug then sucks out the prey's blood. Unlike other assassin bugs, the Malaysian assassin bug puts the empty bodies of ants that it has killed on top of its own body. The dead ants keep away spiders that like to munch on the assassin bugs.

CHAPTER 4

Becoming a Nation

LESS THAN ONE HUNDRED YEARS AGO, NO ONE IN Southeast Asia would have called himself or herself a Malaysian. The people who lived on the Malay Peninsula and northern Borneo were not part of a unified country. Instead, small Muslim kingdoms called sultanates covered much of the region. These sultanates were under the control of Great Britain, which had colonized the country.

Opposite: **Throughout much of history, the people of Sarawak, on the island of Borneo, were isolated from those who lived on the Malay Peninsula.**

Migrations

Long before the British arrived, the area that would become Malaysia was home to many different peoples. Humans and their ancestors have lived in the region for almost two million years. During some of that time, the seas were lower because more of the water on earth was frozen into ice, and a wide swath of land connected Borneo to mainland Asia. When the last ice age ended about twelve thousand years ago and the ice melted into water, the sea level rose, submerging this land. Borneo became an island.

The ancestors of the people who live in Malaysia today did not come to this area in major waves. Instead, there has been a steady stream of migrants over the centuries. This stream began about forty to thirty thousand years ago, when people first began to settle in the interior of the Malay Peninsula. They were the ancestors of the Orang Asli (original people),

An image of Semang people from the early 1900s

Ancient Peoples

Early ancestors of humans lived in the Lenggong Valley, in the state of Perak on the Malay Peninsula, as long as 1.8 million years ago. Scientists have discovered tools these ancient peoples left behind, including the oldest hand axes ever found in Asia.

In 1990, scientists also found a complete human skeleton. Testing shows that "Perak Man" lived about 11,000 years ago. He was buried in a curled-up position, and his remains are the oldest, most-complete human skeleton found in Southeast Asia. Alongside the body were stone tools and grilled animal bones. In 2004, scientists found another skeleton in the region, this time of a woman. "Perak Woman" lived about 3,000 years after Perak Man. Because of the wealth of archaeological findings in this area, in 2012 the Lenggong Valley was named a United Nations Educational, Scientific and Cultural Organization (UNESCO) World Heritage Site. The honor recognizes the importance of the valley in preserving the early history of Malaysia.

the indigenous or native people of the peninsula. The Orang Asli include the Jakun, Semang, and Senoi. The ancestors of today's native peoples of Borneo began arriving there about five thousand years ago. The modern groups include the Iban, Bidayuh, and Kadazan. The native people of East Malaysia are sometimes called Dayaks.

The ancestors of the modern Malay people began arriving in the region about three thousand years ago. They mixed with the indigenous people and later with newcomers from India, China, Persia, and Arab lands of the Middle East.

Building Kingdoms

The Malays had little contact with the outside world until about two thousand years ago, when traders came to the region from India. The Indians came seeking spices, tin, and resources such as hardwoods and rattan—palms that can be woven into furniture. Some Indians stayed and introduced their Hindu religion to the Malays.

With the spread of Indian culture came the first kingdoms on the Malay Peninsula. Some of the kings relied on the Orang Laut (sea people) to help them defend their trade routes. The Orang Laut lived on the eastern Malay Peninsula and were skilled boatbuilders and sailors. They helped fight off pirates and helped promote trade.

Over time, the Srivijaya Empire, based on the island of Sumatra in what is now Indonesia, gained some control over the region. By the thirteenth century, other powers in Southeast Asia also had relationships with the Malay kingdoms.

In about 1400, a prince named Parameswara founded the port of Melaka on the western coast of the Malay Peninsula. Melaka became the base of a great Malay trading empire.

The Rise of Islam

Through trade, Melaka had contact with China, India, and the Philippines. For several decades, trade with China was especially important, and some Chinese settled in Melaka. But by the 1430s, contacts with China weakened. By this time, Parameswara's grand-

Trade Routes in Southeast Asia, 12th Century

- Srivijaya Empire
- Kediri
- — Trade route
- Khmer Empire
- Champa
- — Present-day Malaysia

to China
to India
Indrapura
Angkor
Palembang
Daha

Several historical sources describe the rise of Melaka (left), but these sources don't always agree. Some say that Parameswara (?–1424) was a prince who was living in Sumatra when he declared himself king of the Malays. After leaving Sumatra, he settled first in Singapore and then founded Melaka. A manuscript called the *Malay Annals* tells a different story. It gives the honor of founding Melaka to a prince named Iskandar Shah. One source says he was Parameswara's son, who ruled after his father.

According to one legend, Parameswara chose the location for Melaka while hunting. His dogs flushed a deer out of the forest. Instead of running, the deer stood its ground and fought the dogs. Admiring the deer's courage, Parameswara thought the site would be ideal for his new home. The name Melaka came from a native tree in the region.

son Kechil Besar was in power. Besar was a Muslim and hoped to increase trade with Muslim merchants across Asia. Besar took the name Muhammad Shah, and according to the *Malay Annals*, he ruled well.

Some Malay merchants had already adopted the Muslim religion. Increasingly, people in Melaka and the surrounding islands became Muslims, creating a bond through their shared religion. At the same time, the Malay language was used by traders across the region. Gradually, Melaka gained control of the southern half of the Malay Peninsula, part of Sumatra, and other smaller islands. The Malay language, culture, and religion became dominant in the region.

Melaka Sultanate, 1500

—— Present-day Malaysia

Melaka reached its peak of power around the end of the fifteenth century. The sultanate, or kingdom, weakened as government officials argued with one another. The Melaka sultanate came to an end in the early sixteenth century, with the first arrival of Europeans in the region.

Foreigners Take Control

In 1509, a Portuguese ship sailed into the harbor of Melaka. Starting in the late 1400s, Portugal had sent ships around Africa and then eastward to India and other parts of Asia. They came to trade for precious metals like gold and valuable spices. Many of the spices grew in the islands near the Malay Peninsula. The Malays did not trust the Portuguese and drove them off.

The Portuguese returned two years later with a large fleet, seeking revenge. When the Portuguese came ashore, Sultan Ahmad, the leader of Melaka, rode an elephant into battle against them. The Malays held off the land invasion but finally surrendered after the Portuguese began firing their cannons. The sultan of Melaka fled to the south, where his son founded the sultanate of Johor. Other sultanates were also established throughout the Malay world.

Because of their military might, the Portuguese were able to build a trading post and fort in Melaka, but the Malays continued to fight to retake their city. The Portuguese held Melaka for more than a century, until another European power, the Netherlands, began to assert itself in the region. In 1639, the Dutch united with the Malays of Johor to battle the Portuguese. Together they took Melaka in 1641.

The Dutch dominated trade throughout the region. But during the eighteenth century, they faced competition from the Bugis people. From their homeland of Sulawesi, east of Borneo,

To reach the Malay Peninsula, Dutch ships sailed around Europe, south through the Atlantic Ocean, around the southern tip of Africa, and across the Indian Ocean. The journey took more than six months.

the Bugis moved into Melaka and Borneo. They were fierce fighters and began to take control of sultanates in the region. In 1784, the Dutch defeated the Bugis in battle. But soon they would face a threat from another European nation, Great Britain.

British Power

By the end of the eighteenth century, Great Britain controlled parts of India and was attempting to extend trade even farther east. The trade was carried out by a private company called the East India Company. As the Dutch were fighting the

Traditional Chinese houses and shops fill the streets of George Town.

Bugis, the company was preparing to set up a trading post on Penang, an island in the Strait of Malacca. The first British settlement there, George Town, was founded in 1786.

By the end of the eighteenth century, the East India Company had also taken temporary control of the city of Melaka. Then, in 1819, the British added Singapore to its Malay possessions. In 1824, Singapore, Penang, and Melaka together became known as the Straits Settlements.

Meanwhile, in Sarawak, on the island of Borneo, a British "kingdom" would soon appear. In 1841, James Brooke, a British explorer, helped end a rebellion there against the sultan of Brunei. In return, the sultan gave Brooke control of Sarawak. The Brooke family would rule there until 1946.

George Town
Penang

MALAY
PENINSULA

Dinding

Strait of Malacca

South China Sea

Melaka

SUMATRA

Singapore

Straits Settlements, 1900

——— Present-day Malaysia

Expanding British Influence

The East India Company controlled the Straits Settlements until 1858, when the British government took control. Under the British, thousands of Chinese came to the peninsula and settled in Penang and Singapore to work as merchants and shopkeepers. Other Chinese went to interior Malay sultanates to mine tin. The Chinese mostly kept to themselves, speaking their own language and not adopting Malay culture.

From 1874, the British began to play a more active role in Malay politics, to ensure peace and order. They let the Malays follow the Muslim faith and keep their old ways. But the British sought to control the local governments. British officials called Residents carried out British policies across what came to be called British Malaya.

In 1896, the British combined four peninsular sultanates into the Federated Malay States, with its capital at Kuala Lumpur. Each of the four states still had a sultan, but the British controlled economic decisions. With a united political organization, the British could more easily build railways and organize legal courts. Johor and four other Malay states did not join the new union but remained under British influence. They were known as the Unfederated Malay States. Sabah was also under British control.

Trade and War

Under British rule, Malaya's economy grew, especially after rubber trees were introduced in 1895. Rubber and Malayan tin were sold around the world. But the new wealth went mostly to British and some Chinese merchants. The Malays did not see many benefits from it. They also saw jobs go to Chinese and then Indian immigrants, who flocked to Malaya. Singapore, more than the other Straits Settlements, became an important port for countries trading in Asia, including the United States. Rubber from Malaya passed through the city before going to American factories.

During the 1930s, British colonies across Asia faced a threat from the growing military might of Japan. Starting in 1931, the Japanese took control of part of China, and by 1940 it was clear that Japan wanted to extend its influence over Southeast Asia. On December 7, 1941, Japanese planes attacked U.S. warships at Pearl Harbor, Hawaii. That marked the entry of the United States into World War II. At the same time, Japan attacked sites across Southeast Asia, including Singapore. Within months, the Japanese controlled the Malay Peninsula.

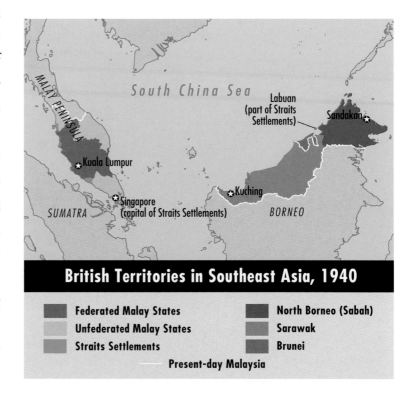

British Territories in Southeast Asia, 1940

- Federated Malay States
- Unfederated Malay States
- Straits Settlements
- North Borneo (Sabah)
- Sarawak
- Brunei
- —— Present-day Malaysia

The war that raged in the Pacific severely disrupted life in Malaya. Trade stopped, and people lacked money to buy food. Japan held Malaya until the war in the Pacific ended in September 1945. The British then returned to power, but some Malays did not want a return to colonialism.

Forming a Country

Before the war, the British had largely agreed to the sultans' wish to keep non-Malays out of the government. After the war, however, the Chinese and Indians wanted government

Japanese soldiers advance across the Malay Peninsula in 1942.

jobs, too. The British saw the need to give non-Malays more rights. In 1948, the Malays and British leaders created the Federation of Malaya, which kept the old political arrangement between the British and the sultans, while preserving the special rights of the Malays. The federation would be a stepping-stone to creating an independent country.

Independence came in 1957. The Chinese and other groups had to accept that the Malays had special rights, and that the government would take extra steps to help them economically. The new country had an elected king, chosen from the nine Malay sultans. In 1963, Singapore, Sarawak, and Sabah joined the federation, which was renamed Malaysia. (Singapore become an independent nation two years later.) Malaysia had valuable natural resources and well-educated government officials. It seemed poised to grow.

Parades wound through the streets when Malaysia became independent in 1957.

The remains of burnt cars lined the streets of Kuala Lumpur's Chinatown following the 1969 riots.

Growth and Challenges

Malaysia did see new wealth come to the country, but much of it went to the Chinese, who still dominated trade and business. Malays struggled to enter a more modern society. Non-Malays had full political rights in the new country, and they created political parties to have more influence over the government. Still, tensions between the Chinese and Malays led to violence in 1969. Thousands of Chinese businesses were burned down and hundreds of people were killed. In the aftermath of the violence, the country focused on strengthening its economy.

Some of the country's greatest growth came under the leadership of Prime Minister Mahathir bin Mohamad, who led Malaysia from 1981 until 2003. During his time in power, manufacturing grew. But Mahathir was also authoritarian, and he had leaders of opposition parties and several members of the Supreme Court arrested. In 1998, he had his deputy prime minister Anwar Ibrahim, who had been challenging his leadership, removed from office and charged with corruption. Many people believed that these charges had no basis, and once Mahathir left office, Anwar was released from prison.

Mahathir bin Mohamad was Malaysia's longest-serving prime minister.

Recent Times

From the founding of Malaysia until the present, a member of the United Malays National Organisation (UMNO) has held the title of prime minister, the leader of the Malaysian government. This party has consistently focused on protecting the legal rights of Malays. Other parties worked to protect the interest of the country's Indians, Chinese, and indigenous people. While the Malays have always held political power, Chinese Malaysians have long had great economic power. In 2010, amid the continuing religious and ethnic divisions

Nurul Izzah Anwar, a member of the People's Justice Party, waves to supporters. The People's Justice Party draws support from people of all ethnic backgrounds.

in the country, Prime Minister Najib Razak announced the 1Malaysia program. Its goal is to create a sense of unity and shared culture among Malaysians of all backgrounds.

Efforts such as this have had mixed success. Malaysia's economy continues to grow, however, and Malayians hope to build on past successes and improve the lives of all the nation's people.

Malaysian prime minister Najib Razak (right) was first elected to Parliament at age twenty-three.

Tragedy

In 2014, Malaysia drew world attention because of two unrelated airplane accidents. In March, a Malaysian Airlines plane carrying 239 people mysteriously disappeared over the Pacific Ocean. Several months later a Malaysian Airlines plane was shot down over Ukraine as a war raged there. Almost 300 people died in that incident.

CHAPTER 5

Government for All

WHEN MALAYSIANS CREATED THEIR OWN government, they borrowed some ideas from the departing British. Like Great Britain, Malaysia is a constitutional monarchy. A monarch—a king or queen—is the chief of state but has little real governmental power. The head of the government in both countries is the prime minister.

Malaysia's history and culture, however, led to some difference with the British system. Unlike Great Britain, Malaysia has individual states, which reflects that Malaysia had independent sultanates within its borders before becoming a country. Malaysia's thirteen states and the national, or federal, government share powers. Malaysia also has three federal

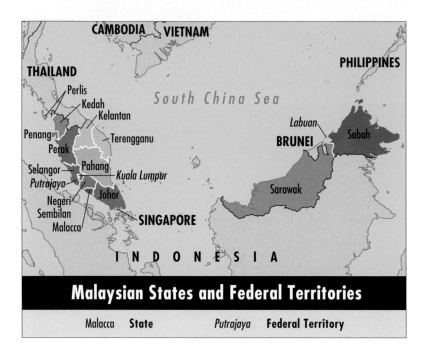

Malaysian States and Federal Territories

| Malacca | **State** | Putrajaya | **Federal Territory** |

territories under the control of the national government. They are Kuala Lumpur, Putrajaya, and Labuan.

Two states, Sarawak and Sabah, have more independence than the other states. They can pass their own sales tax and disregard the advice of some national councils. This kind of independence reflected the attitudes of many residents of those two states before they joined Malaysia in 1963. Chinese and indigenous people in these states did not want to be completely under the control of Malays on the peninsula.

The King and the Conference of Rulers

The king of Malaysia is chosen from the nine sultans in the country, who together make up the Conference of Rulers. The sultans have agreed that the position of king rotates in a set order among them. The Conference of Rulers also elects a deputy head of state who fills in for the king when he is sick, out of the country, or otherwise not able to serve.

The king normally serves for five years. His duties include calling Parliament to session and serving as the supreme commander of Malaysia's military. In some cases, the king can pardon people who have committed crimes.

A Look at Malaysia's Capital

Although Kuala Lumpur is the capital of Malaysia, not all parts of the federal government are located there. The Malaysian Parliament is in Kuala Lumpur, but since 1999, the executive and judicial branches of government have been located in nearby Putrajaya.

During the nineteenth century, Kuala Lumpur, or KL, sprung up in a major tin-producing region near the Klang River. Miners and traders were the first residents, and Chinese immigrants made up a large part of the population. In 1896, the British chose Kuala Lumpur as the capital of the Federated Malay States, which set the city on a path toward becoming the largest city in Malaysia. Its population in 2013 was estimated at 1.7 million.

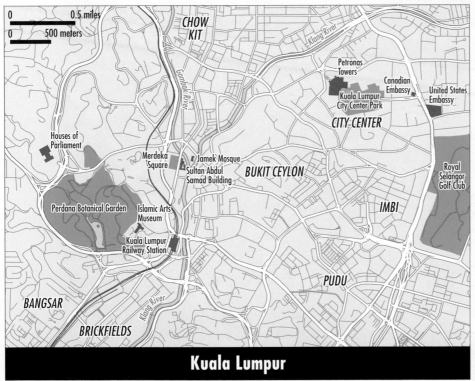

Kuala Lumpur

The city has a vibrant mix of historic and modern buildings. The Sultan Abdul Samad Building (above), which dates from 1897, has a tall clock tower and features architecture influenced by Islamic styles. The Jamek Mosque and the Kuala Lumpur Railway Station also show a mix of Eastern and Western styles. The Petronas Towers, at 1,483 feet, (452 m), were once the world's tallest buildings and are still the world's tallest twin towers. A bridge on the forty-first floor connects the towers and provides a spectacular view of the city.

In Malaysia, religion and government are intertwined. Although the national constitution grants the freedom to worship as one pleases, Islam is the nation's official religion. The head of state must be a Muslim. Nine of the thirteen states have sultans, who are both a political leader and the religious leader in each state. The federal and state governments also fund Islamic schools, a benefit other religions do not receive.

Making the Laws

Malaysia divides its government into three parts, or branches: legislative, executive, and judicial. Parliament is the legislative branch, which means it creates the country's laws. Malaysia's parliament is divided into two sections, or houses, the House of

Malaysian police march in a parade on Independence Day.

The Malaysian Parliament building towers over its neighborhood in Kuala Lumpur.

Representatives and the Senate. The House of Representatives has 222 members who are elected to five-year terms. A member of the House must be a Malaysian citizen and at least twenty-one years old. Only the House can draft proposed laws, called bills, that deal with taxes or spending money.

The Malaysian Senate has seventy members. Senators are not elected. Each state legislature selects two of the senators, and all the rest are appointed by the king. The king is supposed to choose people who have accomplished great

National Government of Malaysia

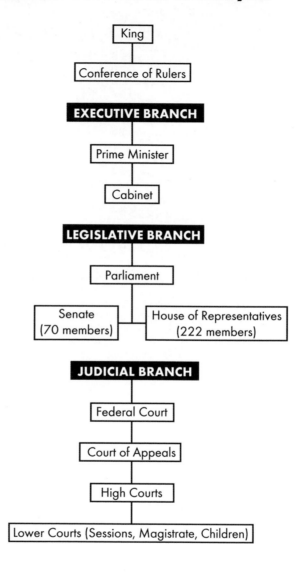

things or represent the interests of indigenous people or other non-Malays. The senators chosen by state legislatures serve three-year terms and a maximum of two terms. Senators must be citizens and at least thirty years old.

After Parliament passes a bill, or proposed law, it goes to the king. The king, however, does not have the power to reject the bill. The king either gives his approval or does not, but either way the bill still becomes law.

The Prime Minister and Cabinet

The executive branch executes, or carries out, the laws. The king is technically the head of this branch, but the executive branch is under the day-to-day control of the prime minister. The prime minister is typically the leader of the political party with the most representatives in the House. Although members of Malaysia's House of Representatives belong to several

Members of Parliament gather to listen to a speech by the king of Malaysia.

different political parties, the dominant party is the United Malays National Organisation (UMNO). All of Malaysia's prime ministers have belonged to the UMNO.

The prime minister chooses the leaders from among the current members of Parliament to lead different executive branch departments. Together, they form the cabinet. The departments in the executive branch include defense, health, agriculture, transportation, and education.

The Judicial System

The judicial branch of government is made up of courts that make sure laws are carried out fairly. The most powerful court

The First Prime Minister

During the 1950s, as the Malayan states were working toward independence, members of wealthy Malay families emerged as political leaders. One member of this elite was Tunku Abdul Rahman (1903–1990). The member of a royal family, he studied at English-language schools on the Malay Peninsula before studying law in England. He became an early leader of the UMNO and encouraged Indian and Chinese parties to work with UMNO for independence. When independence was achieved in 1957, Abdul Rahman became the first prime minister of the new Federation of Malaya. He remained prime minister for more than a decade, but many people were critical of his leadership during the 1969 riots between the Chinese and the Malays, and he was forced to resign the following year. Today, however, he is revered as the father of Malaysian independence.

Malaysia has struggled to elect women to Parliament. In part, that reflects Muslim beliefs about the role of women. Many Muslim men prefer that their wives and daughters stay at home. But some organizations are trying to change Malaysia's attitude toward women.

In 1988, a group called Sisters in Islam, now known as SIS, was founded by Zainah Anwar (left) and others. SIS has worked to promote the rights of Muslim women in Malaysia. It has fought against child marriage and has argued against the government policing the private behavior of Malaysian Muslims. It has also opposed laws that make it illegal for Malaysian Muslims to leave Islam.

Another group, called Empower, was founded in 2008. It has focused on the difficulties Malaysian women face in politics. Along with promoting equal rights for women, Empower has worked to make elections in Malaysia fair. The government controls the press and the voting process, making it hard for outside parties to challenge those in power.

is the Federal Court. It has a chief justice and four other judges. This court hears appeals from lower courts, meaning that someone involved in a case is challenging the lower courts' decision. The Federal Court also advises the king on legal issues and can decide if a federal law violates the constitution.

Below the Federal Court is the Court of Appeals. It also hears appeals from lower courts. Next come the two High Courts, one for the Malay Peninsula and one for the two states in Borneo. The High Courts hear appeals from lower courts

When Malaysians were designing a national flag, they were inspired by another former British colony with a federal form of government—the United States. As with the U.S. flag, alternating red and white stripes fill the Malaysian flag. There are fourteen stripes in all, one for each state and one representing the national government. In the upper left corner of the flag is a blue rectangle. The blue represents the Malay people. Inside the rectangle is a yellow star with fourteen points and a half-moon, or crescent. Yellow is the color associated with Malay rulers. The star represents the unity of the thirteen states and the national government, while the crescent is a symbol of Islam.

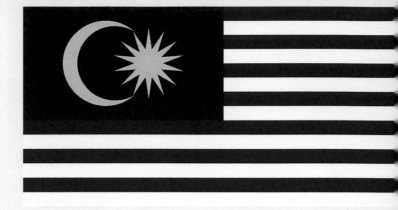

and try all cases involving the death penalty. They also handle some cases involving divorce and custody of children.

Most serious cases are tried in Sessions Courts. There are dozens of Sessions Courts across the country. They can hear all criminal cases unless they involve the death penalty. They also hear civil cases—lawsuits between citizens or companies—that involve large sums of money. Magistrate Courts hear criminal cases with lesser penalties and civil cases involving less money.

States in Malaysia also have their own courts, some of which are religious courts. One type, called syariah (sharia) courts, hears cases involving Muslim family law or religious law. Most syariah cases involve divorce, child custody, inheritance, and similar matters. The states of Sarawak and Sabah have native courts. They hear cases that involve the traditional laws of the indigenous groups who live there.

State and Local Government

The leaders of nine of the states are sultans or kings. Executive duties, however, are carried out by a chief minister chosen by the party that controls the state assembly, the legislature for the state. Four other states have governors who are chosen by the country's king. In these states, too, chief ministers carry

The Federal Court is housed in the majestic Palace of Justice in Putrajaya.

out the executive duties. These ministers rely on a cabinet, just as the prime minister does, to run the executive branch. The three federal territories of Kuala Lumpur, Putrajaya, and Labuan are controlled by the federal government.

The state assemblies create laws for the states, dealing with such things as how money is spent. The state governments also create the local systems of government within the state. Every state has districts with their own councils to run local affairs, such as building roads. Some cities and towns also have their own councils. Council members are chosen by the state government.

Putrajaya is the site of many federal government buildings, including the Ministry of Finance.

The National Anthem

As Malaysia was approaching independence, Malaysian officials created a committee to choose a national anthem for the new country. For the music, the committee chose the tune from the anthem of the Malaysian state of Perak. The music, originally written by a Frenchman named Pierre-Jean de Béranger, had become popular in Perak in the nineteenth century. The committee itself wrote the lyrics. "Negaraku" ("My Country") was adopted as the Malaysian national anthem in 1957.

Malay lyrics

Negaraku

Tanah tumpahnya darahku

Rakyat hidup bersatu dan maju

Rahmat bahagia Tuhan kurniakan

Raja kita selamat bertakhta

Rahmat bahagia Tuhan kurniakan

Raja kita selamat bertakhta.

English translation

My country, my native land

The people living united and progressive

May God bestow His blessings and happiness

May our Ruler have a successful reign

May God bestow His blessings and happiness

May our Ruler have a successful reign.

CHAPTER 6

A Growing Economy

IN DECADES PAST, MOST MALAYSIANS MADE THEIR living off the land, from the sea, or through trade. They grew rice for themselves and other crops to sell overseas. They fished. They mined tin that was shipped around the world. They cut down the hardwood trees of their vast forests to turn into lumber. The work often didn't pay well, and many people faced poverty. During the 1960s, half of all Malaysian households were considered poor.

But starting in the 1970s, the economy of Malaysia began to change. Malaysian natural resources are still in demand around the world, but the growth of industry created more wealth across the country. The country exported more than $230 billion worth of goods in 2014, with its major trading partners being Singapore, China, the United States, and Japan. By 2014, the poverty rate had dropped to just 2 percent.

Opposite: **An employee works on computer circuit boards in a plant on Penang.**

From the Land and Sea

Since Malaysia's economic boom, agriculture, fishing, and logging make up less of the country's gross domestic product (GDP)—the total value of its goods and services produced—than they once did. But rubber and palm oil continue to be in great demand. Malaysia is second only to neighboring Indonesia in producing palm oil, the most commonly used food oil around the world. Date palm plantations make up about 75 percent of all of Malaysia's land used for farming.

A worker hauls away giant clusters of palm oil fruit. Palm oil is extracted from the pulp of the fruit.

Most of the oil comes from the tree's fruit, while some is made from the seed inside the fruit. Growing the trees and producing the oil provides jobs for hundreds of thousands of people. This includes migrants from Indonesia and the Philippines who work under difficult and dangerous conditions for little pay. Malaysia is also a world leader in producing rubber, which is used for car tires and a wide range of other products.

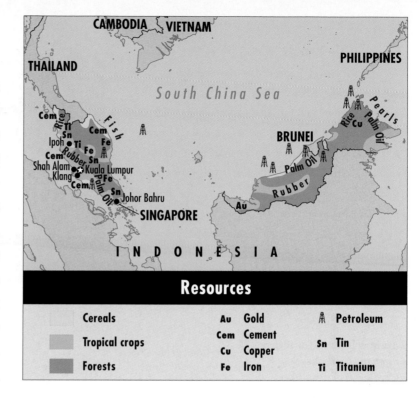

Along with palm oil trees and rubber trees, rice and cocoa beans grow across the country. Pepper, an important spice used in cooking, grows in Sarawak. Mushrooms and honey are produced in Sabah. Other crops grown in Malaysia include coconuts, papayas, pineapples, bananas, and a wide variety of vegetables, such as leafy greens, chili peppers, cucumbers, and cabbage.

Malaysia's farmers also raise a wide range of livestock, including cattle, chickens, and hogs. Malaysia is one of the top producers of duck meat in the world.

Surrounded by ocean waters, Malaysia has a large fishing industry. Much of its fish, however, comes from aquaculture, or fish farms. Some of the farmed fish include shrimp, catfish, and tilapia.

Hungry for More Lobsters

Around the world, lobsters are big business. By some estimates, the market for lobsters is worth $4 billion each year. When the American company Darden Restaurants wanted more lobsters, it came to Sabah, Malaysia. The company spent hundreds of millions of dollars to build the world's first lobster aquaculture park. This park could create up to twelve thousand jobs for Malaysians by 2020, and it shows the country's desire to be a world leader in aquaculture.

In Malaysia's many forests, workers harvest trees in order to use the wood to produce building products, such as plywood, or to make furniture. The forests are also a source of

Bamboo is used for many purposes in Malaysia, including building houses.

bamboo and rattan. Bamboo is an environmentally friendly plant to use as a building material because it grows quickly and can be harvested after only a few years. Hardwood trees, however, grow slowly. It might take a hundred years to grow a new hardwood tree after one has been cut in the rain forest, so cutting many of these trees destroys the forest.

Men work at a tin mine in Ipoh. Until the 1970s, Malaysia was the world's largest producer of tin.

Digging and Drilling

Malaysia once led the world in mining tin, and it remains a major producer of that metal. But today, Malaysian miners dig more iron, gold, and coal than tin. Even more important to the nation's economy is the drilling for petroleum (oil) and natural gas. Malaysia is the world's second-biggest exporter of a liquid form of natural gas and the second-largest producer of oil and natural gas in Southeast Asia. Most of the exploration for these

What Malaysia Grows, Makes, and Mines

AGRICULTURE (2013)

Palm oil	19,200,000 metric tons
Rice	2,600,000 metric tons
Rubber	826,421 metric tons

MANUFACTURING (2012; VALUE OF GOODS)

Semiconductor devices	$16,900,000,000
Industrial chemicals	$9,180,000,000
Computers and related products	$8,760,000,000

MINING

Iron (2012)	10,700,000 metric tons
Oil (2013)	669,000 barrels per day
Natural gas (2013)	2,176,000,000,000 cubic feet

resources is done off the country's coasts. These resources are controlled by a government-owned company called Petronas.

Manufacturing

The growth of Malaysia's economy has come in large part from manufacturing. The country has recruited large foreign companies to open operations, and Malaysians have also started industrial companies. More than one out of every three Malaysians works in manufacturing. The country makes computers and other electronic goods, as well as semiconductors, which are the "brains" of computers and electronic devices.

Malaysians also process the rubber and palm oil into finished products, turn crops into packaged foods, and make a variety of chemicals used in industry and medicines.

Services

In 2012, just over half of Malaysia's GDP came from the service sector of the economy. This includes such businesses as stores, banks, and real estate companies. In recent years, large stores and malls have popped up across the country, especially in the heavily populated region around Kuala Lumpur. Health care, government services, education, and tourism are also part of the service sector of the economy. Every year tourists spend billions of dollars in Malaysia. Direct spending by tourists makes up about 8 percent of Malaysia's GDP. Providing transportation, food, and rooms for those guests creates more than one million jobs.

High-Flying Businessman

Malaysia is encouraging its citizens to become entrepreneurs—businesspeople who take a risk and start their own companies. Young Malaysians have a good model in Tan Sri Tony Fernandes. Trained as an accountant, Fernandes worked and studied in England before returning to Malaysia to work in the music industry. He changed careers from music to the travel industry in 2001, when he and a partner bought a Malaysian airline that had just two old airplanes. Fernandes helped turn AirAsia into a successful company, offering affordable flights across much of Asia on more than 150 planes. For his business skills, Fernandes has won high praise, though the company faced a major setback in December 2014, when one of its jets crashed, killing all 162 people on board.

Moving People and Goods

The ability to move people and goods is an important part of any country's economy. Kuala Lumpur has a large international airport that serves about forty million passengers each year. Several airlines connect cities and larger towns across the country.

Malaysia also has a modern train system and an excellent system of roads. Boats large and small sail between coastal cities and towns and up Malaysia's rivers. Express ferries can carry people at speeds of more than 40 miles (64 km) per hour.

Media

To learn what's going on in the world of art, sports, and entertainment, Malaysians turn to a variety of media. The country has newspapers published in several languages other than Malay,

The Penang Ferry Service is the oldest ferry service in Malaysia. It began operation in 1929.

including English, Chinese, and Tamil. Some newspapers are found only online, such as *Malaysiakini* (*kini* means "now"). The country has both government-owned and privately owned radio and TV stations. Social media has grown increasingly important in Malaysia, because Malaysians, like people the world over, enjoy sharing and gathering information using the Internet. As of 2013, 67 percent of Malaysians used the Internet.

Money in Malaysia

The main unit of currency in Malaysia is the ringgit, which is abbreviated RM. The ringgit is divided into 100 sen. Bills come in values of 1, 2, 5, 10, 20, 50, and 100 ringgit, while coins have values of 5, 10, 20, and 50 sen. The front of all ringgit notes shows the country's first prime minister, Tunku Abdul Rahman. The back of the notes features images of things associated with Malaysia. For example, the back of the 10 ringgit note shows a species of rafflesia flower discovered in Perak in 2003. In 2015, 1 ringgit equaled about US$0.30 and US$1.00 equaled 3.59 ringgit.

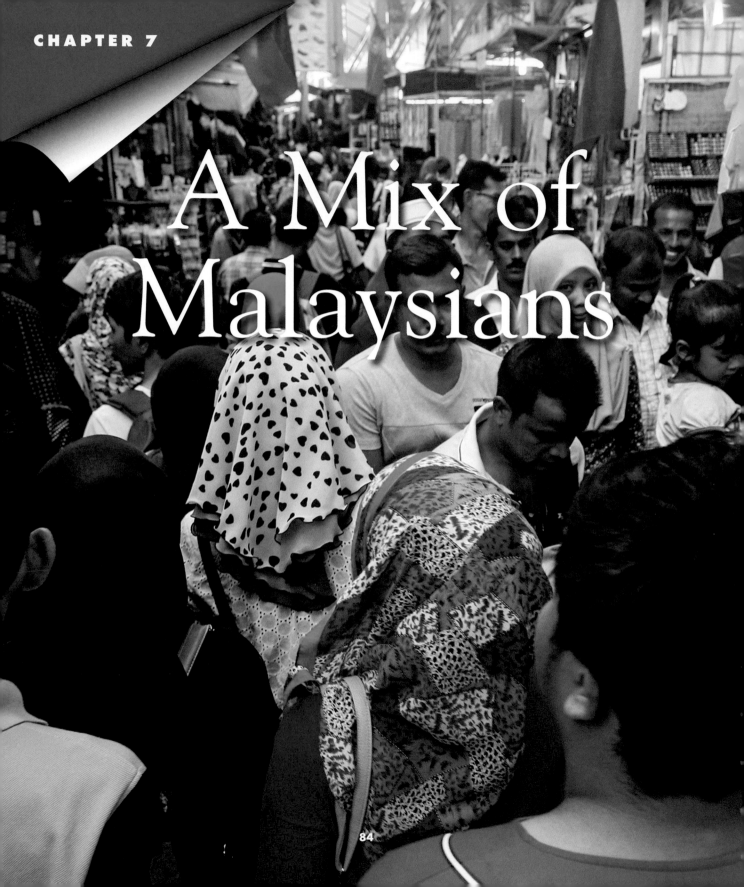

CHAPTER 7

A Mix of Malaysians

Johari Abdullah grew up in Penang, an area that is heavily Chinese, but his family roots are most likely in India or the Middle East. He is Muslim and speaks Malay, but most of his education was in English. Johari knows that ethnic and religious conflicts have erupted in Malaysia over the years. But his life could be a model for the 1Malaysia program the government promotes. He grew up with friends of varied backgrounds. "We visited each other, we played together," he says. "That's the best part of growing up in Malaysia."

In its push to unify all Malaysians, the government created what is called the Unity Squad. Its goal is to get people of all backgrounds working together in their neighborhoods to solve local problems. Leaders of local associations learn special skills to help solve conflicts among members of different ethnic and religious groups. Despite these efforts, much tension remains.

Opposite: **Shoppers crowd a market in Kuala Lumpur.**

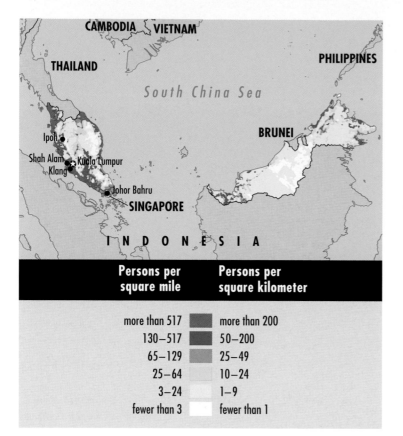

Persons per square mile		Persons per square kilometer
more than 517		more than 200
130–517		50–200
65–129		25–49
25–64		10–24
3–24		1–9
fewer than 3		fewer than 1

A Growing Population

Every ten years, Malaysia conducts a census, or a count of its population. The census also gathers information about where and how the people live. In the last census, taken in 2010, the country's population was 28.3 million. Four years later, the population was estimated to be more than 30 million.

The state with the largest population is Selangor, in West Malaysia. According to the 2010 census, it had nearly 5.5 million people. Kuala Lumpur has the highest density, or the number of people living in an area. In 2010, 17,340 people lived in every square mile (6,696 per sq km) of Kuala Lumpur. The lowest density was in Sarawak, with just 52 people per square mile (20 per sq km).

Since the push to modernize the country began, more Malaysians are leaving small towns and villages in rural areas and moving to larger towns and cities. In 2010, 71 percent of the people lived in urban areas, compared to less than half that number in 1980. Literacy—the ability to read and write—is also increasing. In 1980, less than 80 percent of the adult population was literate. By 2010, the literacy rate had risen to 97 percent.

Population of Major Cities (2011 est.)	
Kuala Lumpur	1.6 million
Klang	1.2 million
Johor Bahru	1 million
Ipoh	700,000
Shah Alam	670,000

Ethnic Groups

Malaysia's constitution spells out who is a Malay. People who practice Islam, speak Malay, and follow Malay customs are Malays. The distinction becomes important in daily life, as Malays receive special privileges from the government. Some programs are designed to give Malays help in starting businesses or getting government jobs. Malays have long resented the power ethnically Chinese Malaysians have in the business world.

The Malays of Malaysia have a special name for themselves and other indigenous groups. Together, they are called

Children in a village in Sabah. About 30 percent of the people in Malaysia are under age fifteen.

Bumiputera—"sons of the soil." These include the Orang Asli of the peninsula and native people of East Malaysia. Together, the Bumiputera make up two-thirds of the population.

The Malay are easily the largest ethnic group in the country, making up just over half of the population. Next come the Chinese, then non-Malay Bumiputera, and Indians. East Malaysia has a much larger number of indigenous non-Malays. In Sarawak, the 2010 census found that Ibans made up 30 percent of the population, while in neighboring Sabah, the Kadazan and related Dusun made up almost 25 percent of the population.

Ethnic Chinese people performing morning tai chi exercises near Kuala Lumpur

Within certain ethnic groups, there can be other divisions. In Malaysia, the term "Indian" applies to people who come from India, Pakistan, or Sri Lanka. Among the Indians are a number of people who trace their roots to Tamil Nadu, a state in southern India. Many Malaysian Tamils keep alive their own language and culture. These are usually Tamil who practice Hinduism. Others, however, are Muslim and identify themselves with the majority of Malays.

Within the Chinese community, there is a group called the Peranakans. They trace their roots to Chinese traders who came to Melaka starting as early as the fourteenth century. They stayed and married Malay women and adopted some

More than two million people of Indian descent live in Malaysia.

Ethnic Groups of Malaysia

Bumiputera (Malays and indigenous people)	67.4%
Chinese	24.6%
Indians	7.3%
Others	0.7%

A Vanishing People

As a girl, Iton Lasah endured great pain as elders from her village tattooed her hands and feet. This ritual symbolized that she was ready for adulthood and to endure the pain of childbirth. All Sekapan girls once went through this, but the tradition of tattooing them has died out. Some people worry the Sekapans might die out, too.

In 2012, there were only about two thousand of them left in Sarawak. The number of Sekapan people is diminishing because today they sometimes marry Chinese or indigenous people from other groups and leave their villages. Younger Sekapans see themselves as Malaysians rather than as members of an indigenous group, and they are not as connected to the old ways. Some Sekapans, though, want to keep their traditional ways and remain in their villages. The government has promised to spend money in the region to help this ethnic group survive.

Malay customs. Some moved on to Penang and Singapore and were sometimes called Straits Chinese. The Chinese community is also divided because some people speak different dialects, or versions, of Chinese. For example, in Penang, there are some Hokkien speakers, while many Chinese in Kuala Lumpur speak Cantonese.

Most residents of Malaysia are also citizens of the country, but the 2010 census found that about 8 percent of the population was not. Many of the noncitizens are foreigners who come to Malaysia for work. These migrant workers come from a variety of Asian countries, including Vietnam, Indonesia, the Philippines, Nepal, India, and Myanmar.

The Languages of Malaysia

According to the Malaysian constitution, Malay is the nation's official language. The language is also spoken in neighboring Brunei, Indonesia, and Singapore. Despite the official status of Malay, English is widely spoken across the country. Most government documents are printed in both Malay and English, and

English is widely used in business. Young people think of English as an international language that would be useful to speak, and English is used in many private schools. Other languages spoken in Malaysia include different forms of Chinese, Tamil and other Indian languages, indigenous languages, and Thai.

Many migrant workers in Malaysia are employed in the construction industry.

What's in a Name?

When North Americans introduce themselves or write their names, they use their first name followed by their family name, or surname. Malaysians are a little different. They use their father's first name instead of a surname after their first name. Some Muslims also put *bin* or *binti* in between the two names. These mean, respectively, "son of" and "daughter of." When Malay women marry, they keep their own name, rather than taking their husband's name. Chinese Malaysians do use a family name, but it comes before their given name. A Christian Chinese may add an English name before his or her Chinese name. Indian names are like the Malay names. Some Malaysians also have titles, which are given by the government. These titles include Dato', Datuk, or Tan Sri, and mean something similar to "sir" or "lord."

Speaking Malay

Here are some common phrases in Malay and their meanings in English:

Ya	Yes
Tidak	No
Helo	Hello
Selamat tinggal	Good-bye
Silakan	Please
Terima kasih	Thank you
Sama-sama	You're welcome
Apa kabar?	How are you?
Kabar baik	I'm fine
Nama saya...	My name is...

A sign in Bako National Park is written in both Malay and English.

The Malay language is usually written with the Latin alphabet, the same alphabet used to write English. This writ-

The jawi alphabet is so fluid and elegant it is frequently used in art.

ten alphabet is called Rumi. But Malays also have their own written alphabet. The earliest was based on a writing system used in India. Later, the Malays adopted a written alphabet similar to one used in Arab countries. Today, that alphabet, called *jawi*, is still sometimes used, especially in newspapers.

From Malay to English

Dutch and British people living and working in colonial Malaya adopted some Malay words. Here are some still used in English today.

Malay	English
amok	amok (crazy or violent state of mind)
bamboo	bamboo
gekok	gecko (type of lizard)
kakatua	cockatoo (bird)
kampung	compound (group of buildings)
kutu	cooties
orang hutan	orangutan
sarung	sarong (type of women's clothing)

CHAPTER 8

Many Spiritual Paths

FROM THE CROWDED STREETS OF KUALA LUMPUR TO remote villages, a voice rings out five times day. Loudspeakers at mosques across Malaysia broadcast the *adhan*, a call to prayer, and the faithful stop their daily activities to follow it.

Under the Malaysian constitution, Malaysia is an Islamic nation, and to be considered a Malay, a person must be a Muslim. But the constitution also guarantees freedom of religion, so a wide range of faiths are practiced. Even within the Muslim community, people have different views about the role the faith should play in the country.

Traditional Religions

Before Indian, Chinese, and Arab traders brought their religions to what became Malaysia, native people had local religions and practices. Like followers of most religions, the

Religion in Malaysia	
Islam	61.3%
Buddhism	19.8%
Christianity	9.2%
Hinduism	6.3%
Other religions	1.7%
Unknown	1.0%
No religion	0.7%

indigenous Malaysians believed that people have a soul that continues on after death. Many indigenous groups had rituals intended to help them stay in contact with the souls of their relatives who had died. Some sites in Malaysia had great meaning to the indigenous people of the region. For example, some people in the highlands of Sarawak consider Mount Murud to have religious importance.

Today, some indigenous people in Malaysia maintain their traditional practices only, while others combine elements of their traditional religion with elements of another religion.

Members of the Mah Meri group perform a dance at a ritual thanking the sea for its bounty.

Islam

Of the many faiths that were brought to Malaysia, Islam is the most important today. Muslims believe that Muhammad, the founder of the religion, communicated with God, whom they call Allah. This is the same God that Christians and Jews wor-

A man prays at a mosque in Malaysia.

The Blue Mosque

In Shah Alam, just outside Kuala Lumpur, as many as twenty-four thousand people can worship inside the Blue Mosque. The largest mosque in Malaysia, it was completed in 1988. Its official name is the Sultan Salahuddin Abdul Aziz Shah Mosque. Its much shorter nickname refers to the building's large blue and silver dome. Inside the building, blue stained-glass windows create a bluish tint during the daytime. The mosque's four minarets are each 466 feet (142 m) tall and were once the tallest minarets in the world.

Many Spiritual Paths   **97**

ship. But Muslims believe that Muhammad received the last, true ideas on how people should worship God. The communications Muhammad is said to have received from God were compiled to form the Muslim holy book, the Qur'an.

Practicing Muslims typically pray five times a day, always facing in the direction of Mecca, Saudi Arabia, Islam's holiest city. Devout Muslims also follow other religious rules. They do not eat pork or drink alcohol.

Malaysia has laws to protect Islam as the state religion. Members of other faiths cannot try to make Muslims give up their faith to follow another religion. And in the early 2000s, the government made it illegal in some cases to use the word *Allah* to refer to God in Christian contexts. This posed a problem for Christians who speak Malay and have always used *Allah* to refer to God.

Islamic Astronaut

Dr. Sheikh Muszaphar Shukor is a scientist, an astronaut, and a practicing Muslim. In 2007, Shukor became the first Malaysian to enter space when he traveled to the International Space Station, a research laboratory that has been operating in orbit around earth since the year 2000. During Shukor's time working in the space station, he continued with his daily prayers. He made sure to face Earth, even if he couldn't exactly face Mecca. Since there is no gravity in the space station, Shukor had to strap his feet down to pray. His trip led Islamic officials in Malaysia to draft special rules for Muslims to follow when they visit the space station.

Malaysia's Muslims sometimes have different views on important issues. Some Muslim women, for example, do not like the restrictions men have placed on their activities. And some Muslims ignore the rules against drinking alcohol and eating pork.

Malaysian Hindus pray at a temple during Navratri, a major Hindu festival that lasts for nine nights.

Hinduism

The first major foreign religion to reach the Malay Peninsula was Hinduism. Indian traders brought it to the region, and

The Cave Temple

Just outside Kuala Lumpur are the Batu Caves, which contain one of the most important holy sites for Malaysia's Hindus. A wealthy Tamil Indian founded a temple inside the Batu Caves in 1891, and hundreds of thousands of Hindus still gather there to celebrate Thaipusam, an elaborate festival in honor of the Hindu deity Murugan. A golden statue of Murugan, 141 feet (43 m) tall, stands in front of the 272 steps that lead up to the Temple Cave. The Temple Cave features many statues of Hindu deities, and its ceiling is covered with paintings of scenes from Hindu holy books.

some ruling Malays adopted it. Hindus believe in a number of gods and in the idea of reincarnation, or that a person's soul or spirit is reborn after death. More Hindus from India came to the region when it was a British colony.

Sikhs also came from India to what is now Malaysia. Like Hindus, Sikhs believe in reincarnation, but they believe in just one god and reject the role of religious rituals.

A Sikh man at a temple in Johor. Sikh men typically wear turbans over their hair.

The Buddha

More than 2,500 years ago, an Indian prince named Siddhartha Gautama (ca. 563-ca. 483 BCE) walked away from his family's riches to seek the meaning of life. He had studied the Vedas, religious writings that shaped Hinduism. He knew about reincarnation and the idea of karma—that what people do, good or bad, influences what happens to them later in this life and in other lives. Siddhartha spent years meditating before achieving what Buddhists now call an awakening. Siddhartha became known as the Buddha, which means "enlightened one." He realized that through meditation, by letting go of the desire for material objects, and by understanding suffering anyone could be enlightened. People who have become enlightened have reached a state of nirvana, which is beyond suffering and free from the cycle of death and rebirth that is part of reincarnation. The Buddha spread his message across northern India, and the people he taught spread it even farther. These spiritual ideas eventually reached China, and the Chinese took them to Malaysia. Today, Buddhism is practiced around the world.

Buddhism and Daoism

The next major faith to reach Malaysia was Buddhism, which also has its roots in India. The number of Buddhists in Malaysia was small until Chinese immigrants came to work on Malaya and Borneo during the nineteenth century. Buddhism teaches that human suffering arises from desire, and that people can overcome suffering by letting go of desire for worldly goods. Many Chinese also subscribe to Daoism, a philosophy that encourages people to maintain harmony in their existence.

Christianity

When the Portuguese came to Malaysia, they tried to convert the local people to Christianity, but they mostly failed. Their brutal way of taking control and holding power did not convince many people to adopt Christianity. The Dutch

Christians sing at a Methodist church in Kuala Lumpur. Methodism is the largest Protestant denomination in Malaysia.

also spread Christian teachings, and a church they built in Melaka still stands. The Roman Catholic Church had a presence in Penang in 1810, and later in that century, Protestant missionaries had some success converting indigenous people to Christianity, especially in what became East Malaysia. Some immigrants from India and China were also practicing Christians when they came to Malaysia.

Today, most Malaysian Christians live in East Malaysia. Across the country, Catholics, Protestants, and members of the Orthodox Church represent the many forms of Christianity. There are about one million Catholics in Malaysia, making them the largest Christian group in the country. The largest Protestant denominations are Methodists, Anglicans, and Lutherans. Most Christian churches in the country belong to the Christian Federation of Malaysia. Its goals include working with members of other faiths while also protecting the rights of Christians to worship freely.

CHAPTER 9

Creating and Playing

The streets and markets of Malaysia's cities offer a colorful feast for the eyes, thanks to some of the batik fabric on display. Decorating fabrics using wax or threads of silver goes back hundreds of years in the country. So does carving items out of wood. Old forms of art are still popular across Malaysia. As with much of Malaysia's culture, the arts of indigenous Malays and other peoples have often been shaped by traditions from other parts of Asia and from Europe.

Ancient Fabrics for Today

For the indigenous people of Malaysia, crafts once provided them with all the items they needed for daily life. These included clay and metal pots, knives, and fabrics. Carvers, especially in Borneo, made wooden masks and other items with religious importance. Some of the handcrafted items, such as jewelry, were also made for the wealthy.

Today, these artistic traditions continue. Many people believe that the best batik comes from the eastern side of the Malay Peninsula. To create batik, the cloth maker draws patterns or images, such as of plants or butterflies, with wax, which prevents the area from taking on the color of the dye applied to the fabric. Adding wax to different areas and then applying different dyes creates colorful patterns.

Another typically Malaysian cloth is songket. The weaver adds gold or silver threads to cotton or silk, though today

Flowers and leaves are the most common decoration used in Malaysian batik.

Wooden masks for sale in Melaka

threads the color of gold or silver are more common than the actual metals. In the past, only members of royal families wore clothes made from songket. Today, anyone can wear it, though usually people wear songket only for special occasions.

Art from Wood and Metal

In a country filled with forests, it is no surprise that carving wood is a Malaysian art form. Some of the best carvers are in Sabah and Sarawak. Carvers create masks with frightening faces, which are supposed to keep away evil spirits. Iban men once used large, elaborately carved wooden shields when they went into battle. Today the shields are prized for the designs carved into them.

A Powerful Knife

Some metalsmiths in Malaysia make a curved knife called a *keris*. While modern kerises are more for show, Malays once used them in battle. The blade of a keris typically has a wavy edge, rather than the straight edge most knives have. In the past, the number of waves in the blade indicated the owner's social position. A sultan's keris had nine waves. Some Malays once believed that kerises had special powers. For example, a person could harm enemies by jabbing the knife into their footprints. The most famous keris belonged to the legendary warrior Hang Tuah. It was said to have magical powers that protected him in battle. Today, a keris might be worn on a belt during special ceremonies, such as a marriage.

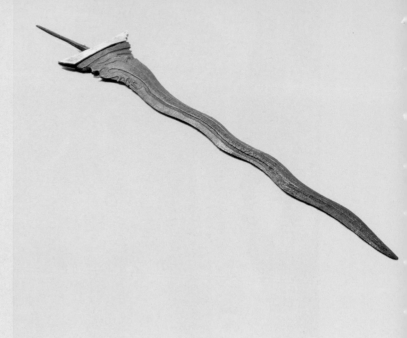

Many old art forms are in danger of dying out because few people today need handcrafted items or want to learn the skills. Still, some crafts such as metalworking continue. Metal goods are usually made in silver or bronze and include dinnerware covered with detailed designs. In Sabah, some villages are known for their metal gongs. The large ones made for religious ceremonies can be 6 feet (1.8 m) wide. Tattooing using traditional designs is also growing in popularity.

Traditional Music

In the sixteenth century, a royal instrumental ensemble called the *nobat* developed. This group played only for sultans at important ceremonies. The nobat included drums, oboes, and gongs.

Gamelan is another type of instrumental music. It is usually associated with Indonesia, but a form of it developed in Malaysia, too. The musicians play wood and metal xylophones, gongs, and a large drum called a *gendang*. Traditional Malaysian music features drums of different sizes, as well as flutes, trumpets, and the *rebab*, a stringed instrument played with a bow.

The Written Word

The oldest known writings in the Malay language are more than 1,300 years old. Some told the stories of great kings and heroes.

Modern Malaysian writers have made a mark around the world. Shahnon Ahmad has been both a politician and a novelist, and his work frequently deals with social and political issues. His novel *Ranjau Sepanjang Jalan* (1966) was adapted into a film called *Rice People*. Muhammad Salleh is considered one of Malaysia's greatest poets. Novelists Tash Aw and Tan Twan Eng, both of whom write in English, have been finalists for major international literary prizes. Aw's *The*

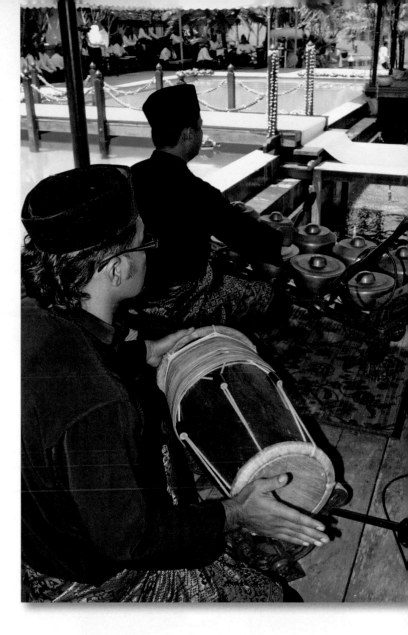

Malaysian musicians play traditional gamelan music.

The Art of Islam

The Arab and Persian traders who brought Islam to Malaysia also brought examples of Islamic art. Today, some of that art is on display in Kuala Lumpur's Islamic Arts Museum. Opened in 1998, the museum features more than seven thousand pieces of art from Muslim countries around the world. The items on display include coins, carpets, the written orders of sultans, models of some of the world's most famous mosques, and jewelry. The museum's arms and armor collection has many ancient swords, shields, and armor with beautiful designs etched into them. Along with art, the museum houses a library for children, where they can learn more about Islamic art and ideas.

Harmony Silk Factory won the Commonwealth Writers' Prize for Best First Novel in 2005. Eng's *The Gift of Rain* has been translated into several other languages.

Another writer is Kee Thuan Chye. Malaysians know him for his articles about politics. He has also written poetry and plays, and has appeared as an actor on TV shows and in movies.

Tan Twan Eng won the 2012 Man Asian Literary Prize for his novel *The Garden of Evening Mists*.

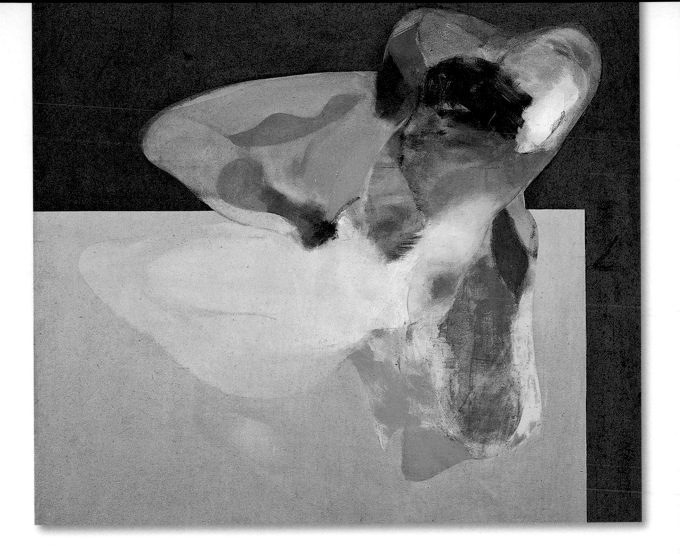

The World of Art

Malaysian visual art, such as paintings, often reflect both Asian and Western influences. Ibrahim Hussein, the country's most famous artist, painted scenes from Malay life using techniques from Western art, such as collage. He worked in bright colors, influenced by the dyes used in batik fabrics. Another highly praised artist is Latiff Mohidin. He had his first art show when he was just ten years old, and he uses colors to express impressions, rather than the world as it really is.

A work by Ibrahim Hussein, the first Malaysian artist to achieve major international recognition. Hussein's work was often soft and fluid.

People Like Lat

Drawing cartoons well requires great skill, and one of the best cartoonists is Mohammad Nor Khalid, who is better known as Lat. He began drawing political cartoons during the 1970s, depicting people from all walks of life. The cartoons first appeared in a Malaysian newspaper, but over time they were collected into books. He also published a graphic novel called *Kampung Boy*. The book describes his experiences growing up during the 1950s as a Muslim in a small Malaysian village. Lat used black-and-white drawings and simple text to tell his tale. The book, which was popular in Southeast Asia, was released in North America in 2006.

The architecture of Malaysia combines aspects of building design from many other countries. Malaysia's temples and mosques, for example, reflect the architecture of China, India, and Arab nations. One local architectural style comes from the Minangkabau people of the western Malay Peninsula. Their traditional houses have steep roofs that end in a point. The roofs are meant to look like the horns of a water buffalo. Some modern buildings in the state of Negeri Sembilan have this distinctive design as well.

Popular Culture

Many Malaysians have made their mark in the world of popular culture. Michelle Yeoh wanted to be a dancer, but she ended up a film actor, often appearing in martial arts movies. She was featured in the James Bond film *Tomorrow Never Dies* and in the ancient epic *Crouching Tiger, Hidden Dragon*, which won film awards around the world. Yeoh also starred in the sequel, which came out in 2015.

Considered a Malaysian treasure, though less well known outside of the country, actor P. Ramlee starred in dozens of Malay films in the 1950s and 1960s. He also wrote movie screenplays and sometimes the music for them as well. Ramlee also sang some of the songs he wrote.

Singing stars in Malaysia include Adibah Noor, who is also a radio broadcaster, and jazz singer Sheila Majid, who is popular in Indonesia as well.

Two Malaysian men have won fame in the world of fashion design. Zang Toi went from a small Malaysian village to New York City, where he learned how to design clothes. Now his fashions are known around the world. Although he lives in the United States, Zang is still a Malaysian citizen. Jimmy

A New Voice

In just a short time, the singer and songwriter Yuna (1986–), whose full name is Yunalis Mat Zara'ai, has gone from performing in small clubs in Kuala Lumpur to appearing on U.S. television. Yuna's music mixes soul and pop. After winning several musical awards in her homeland, Yuna moved to the United States to record the album *Nocturnal*, which was released in 2013. As a follower of Islam, Yuna wears a hijab, a traditional head covering for Muslim women. She has been called the leader of a new movement among some young Muslim women in Malaysia. They openly show their faith while seeking personal independence.

When it comes to women's squash, no one has dominated the game like Nicol David. At age fifteen, she won a gold medal at the 1998 Asian Games, a sporting event held every four years for Asian athletes. David won gold again in 2006, 2010, and 2014, and from 2006 through 2014 she was the top-ranked women's squash player in the world. In 2010, she didn't lose a single match the entire season as she played in tournaments around the world. David's next goal is to see women's squash made an Olympic sport. To help achieve that, she started Squash Stars, which uses social media to draw attention to the sport. Though she travels the world playing squash, David loves to return home, where people treat her as a sports superstar.

Choo has found similar success designing shoes. His father was a shoemaker, and Choo started out by learning that trade. His first shoes were handmade for wealthy customers, but then he began designing and selling shoes anyone could buy. Today he trains people in the skill of shoemaking.

On the Playing Field

Many of the most popular sports in Malaysia came to the country with the British. These sports include soccer (called football), field hockey, cricket, and rugby. Two top sports are the racket games badminton and squash. Malaysia has produced some of the world's best badminton players, such as Tan Aik Huang, Lee Chong Wei, and Razif Sidek.

Boys play soccer on a soggy field in Kuala Lumpur.

Kite-flying might not seem like much of a sport to North Americans, but this traditional pastime is taken seriously in Malaysia. Each year, Johor hosts one of the world's best international kite festivals, drawing hundreds of flyers from around the world.

Go Fly a Wau Bulan

Malaysia is home to a kind of kite called a *wau bulan*. *Wau* is pronounced like "wow," and that's what many English speakers say when they see these beautiful kites. Wau is the Malaysian word for kite because the basic kites of the country are said to look like an Arabic letter called wau. *Bulan* means moon. A wau bulan features a crescent shape, like a partial moon. Kitemakers cut out brightly colored pieces of paper to decorate the kites, which have bamboo frames. A wau bulan can be huge. Some are 9 feet (2.7 m) wide and 12 feet (3.6 m) tall.

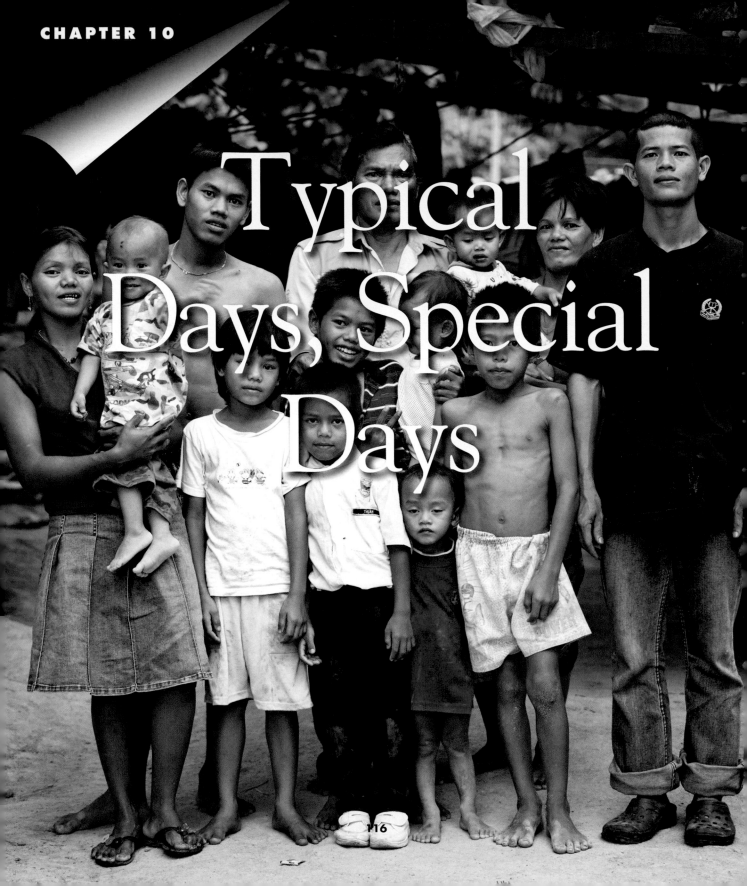

CHAPTER 10

Typical Days, Special Days

116

In an apartment in Kuala Lumpur, a family prepares to head out on a typical weekday. Both parents work for a foreign company with an office in the city. The children catch a bus to head off to school. When the day is done, the family gathers for a meal, after which the children do their homework.

The daily routine is different for a rural family in Sabah. In the countryside, a mother is less likely to work outside the home, and she spends her days taking care of the house and preparing meals. For kids, getting to school might mean a walk down a dirt road.

For Malaysians, family is their top priority. Children are taught to respect adults, especially adult relatives. The idea of saving face—not doing something to embarrass others in public—is very important. Malaysians are friendly and treat visitors well. In return, visitors to someone's home almost always bring a gift.

Opposite: **Friends and family in rural Malaysia. The average Malaysian family has two or three children.**

A Child's Life

Daily life for most children in Malaysia revolves around school. Schools meet almost year-round. The government has established public schools, but many children go to private schools that teach in languages other than Malay, such as Chinese and English. Regardless of the kind of school they attend, students wear uniforms. Boys typically wear dark pants or shorts and blue or white shirts. Girls usually wear white tops with a blue dress or a skirt. Muslim girls usually wear a headscarf. After school, some students take part in sports or

Students in a class in Peninsular Malaysia. Many classes in Malaysia are large, with forty or more students.

other activities. Some families also pay for their children to have private tutoring outside of school.

Children can begin attending preschool at three or four years of age. After that, they attend primary school for six years. Most students then go on to secondary school—what would be middle school and high school in North America. Each year of secondary school is called a form. Form 5 is typically the last year of secondary school, though some students continue studying before going to college.

Despite a long school year, children do have time for fun. Since most of the country is hot throughout the year, children and their families often seek indoor activities in air-conditioning. That can mean shopping at a mall or playing in an indoor sports center. And, of course, swimming in pools or the nearby ocean also offers relief from the constant heat.

Big on Gasing

Spinning a top is a fun activity for children around the world. But for Malaysians, tops are not just child's play. Adults also compete in events with tops.

In Malaysia, the top itself and the act of spinning it are both called *gasing*. Wooden tops made for children are usually small and come in different shapes. Some look like hearts or eggs, while others have flat tops. A string is wrapped around the gasing's top. The child then launches it by flinging it out while holding on to the end of the string. The goal is to see who can spin the top the longest. In another gasing game, one player tries to knock another player's top out of a circle on the ground.

The gasings adults use in competition are much larger—some can weigh 10 pounds (4.5 kg). With the proper skill, a player can launch a top that spins for more than ninety minutes!

At Home

As in other countries, Malaysians do not have just one kind of housing. City families might live in modern apartment buildings. In suburbs, families might have a small home of their own. In Penang or Melaka, Chinese families with small businesses sometimes live on the top floor of their shophouses. These narrow buildings are crammed together in older neighborhoods. Some of these buildings date to the eighteenth century.

The traditional Malay home in a *kampung*, or village, is built on stilts. This helps cool the house and keeps it safe when there are floods. The frame is made of wood, and either wood or plants are used for the walls. The roofs are traditionally thatch, dried reeds, or straw. The kitchen is located at the back of the house and can be separated from the main part of the house by a small, open porch. Coconut trees often line walkways outside to provide shade—and coconuts.

What to Wear

Malaysians wear many different styles of clothes. In cities, some men wear suits to work, while women wear dresses. At night, they and their families might relax in jeans and T-shirts.

Other people wear clothing associated with their ethnic group. For a Malay woman, the typical blouse is called a *baju kurung*. It has long sleeves and reaches to a woman's knees. It can come in many colors and is worn with a long skirt.

The Longhouse

One striking kind of house found in rural areas of East Malaysia is the longhouse. This long, wooden structure was traditionally built by indigenous peoples along riverbanks, though the Bidayuh of Sarawak built theirs near hills. A longhouse sits on stilts, and a family's farm animals typically stay under the house in the shade. Related families live together in the longhouse. They share a common area while also having private rooms. In the past, longhouses were covered with thatch, but today they usually have metal roofs.

Some foreign visitors enjoy spending a night at a longhouse. Women sleep inside, while the men stay in a long, covered outdoor area called a veranda. Across Malaysia, the government promotes this homestay program, which lets foreigners experience daily life in small villages.

The Hats of Malaysia

Malaysians frequently wear hats and wraps on their heads. Some Muslim women wear a headscarf or covering called a *hijab*. The hijab wraps around the head and falls down across the shoulders. For Malay men, the trademark hat is the *songkok*. Not quite a perfect circle, this short hat usually has a flat top. In Sarawak, skilled craftspeople make traditional hats that are covered with colorful beads. Kadazan women are known for their straw hats. Sikhs wear a wrapped fabric turban called a *dastar*. The Bajau men of Sabah also wear a hat of that name, though it stands taller on the head and often has many colors.

A sarong, a long skirt wrapped around the waist, is worn by women across Malaysia. Malay men wear a long shirt called a *baju melayu* and pants. Sometimes they wrap a short sarong called a *sampin* over the pants. Chinese women favor a long dress with a high collar called a *cheongsam*. Indian women wear a large piece of fabric called a sari that is wrapped around their body and over their left shoulder.

Clothes tend to be lightweight and loose, because of the warm climate. In remote villages, people still wear traditional clothing for special events. This can include headdresses with feathers or clothing made from threads taken from tree bark.

Fantastic Foods

Malaysia is famous for its varied foods, the result of the blending of so many cultures. George Town, in Penang, has been called the country's food capital. The smell of foods sizzling

A woman in traditional dress rides a scooter in Johor.

in pans fills the streets. Streetside cooks combine ingredients from the country's many ethnic groups and use their various cooking methods to make dishes that they then sell to eager eaters strolling by.

Promoting Malaysian Cooking

He's on TV and the Internet, and his cookbooks are sold around the world. He's Redzuawan Ismail, who is better known as Chef Wan. Trained as an accountant, Wan began working as a chef more than twenty years ago. As a boy, he sold his mother's *guay* cakes—Chinese rice cakes—to soldiers at a local military base. As an adult, he studied cooking in the United States and France before returning to Malaysia. He has traveled around the world to introduce people to the variety of Malaysian foods he enjoys. In 2010, the government made him Malaysia's food ambassador to the world.

Noodles are a popular street food in Malaysia.

The dishes include curries, which are a combination of many different spices, coconut milk, and a mixture of meats and vegetables. One popular dish in Penang and other parts of Malaysia is *char koay teow*, which features rice noodles stir-fried with shrimp, other seafood, sausage, bean sprouts, and soy sauce.

Typical meats in Malaysian stir-fries include lamb, beef, chicken, or seafood. Some dishes contain pork. *Satay* is a meal of grilled meat served on a stick. For people who do not eat certain meats, such as devout Muslims who do not eat pork, and devout Hindus who do not eat beef, there are many alternatives. Many vegetarians eat a meat substitute called tempeh, which is made from soybeans.

Malaysians eat lots of rice, and some of it comes in a dish called *nasi lemak.* The rice is cooked in coconut milk, and then diners add other items to it, such as peanuts, meat, vegetables, or eggs. Nasi lemak was traditionally a breakfast food, but Malaysians now eat it any time of day. Many dishes, especially those with Chinese influences, feature noodles. Sauces for foods often begin with a spicy paste called *sambal*, and combine different spices and sometimes bits of shrimp.

In rural areas, people often eat tapioca or sago, a kind of starch, instead of rice. Their meat sometimes comes from wild animals, such as deer or boars, and they catch and cook their own fish.

Nasi lemak is considered the national dish of Malaysia.

Colorful lion dancers are part of Chinese New Year celebrations in Malaysia.

Celebrating Together

Along with religious and national holidays, some special events, such as a birth or a wedding, call for celebration. The feast served to mark these days is called a *kenduri*. In rural areas, the female members of a family sometimes cook for several days to prepare the feast, which is shared with neighbors. The neighbors sometimes help cook, too, knowing they'll get the same help when it's their turn to host a kenduri.

National Holidays

Many public holidays in Malaysia are religious, but Malaysians also celebrate some nonreligious holidays.

Chinese New Year	January or February
Labor Day	May 1
King's Birthday	First Saturday in June
National/Independence Day	August 31
Malaysia Day	September 16

Many Ways to Marry

Of all the Malaysian events that might feature a feast, a wedding is the most important. Weddings can be performed in a religious setting or in a government office, and they vary greatly depending on the background of the people getting married.

For Muslims, adult relatives from the man's and woman's families once arranged a marriage. This is not common today. Couples planning to marry announce their engagement and then exchange gifts. The night before the wedding, the couple has a small religious ceremony. The couple signs a contract. The more festive and public wedding takes place the next day.

In Chinese communities, families of the couple exchange gifts up to three weeks before the wedding. The groom also pays a "bride price," some amount of money or property, to the bride's family. Traditionally, three days after the wedding, a groom gave his new bride's family a roasted pig. The family cut out part of the pig and ate it. They then returned the rest of the pig to the groom's family with several small gifts wrapped in red—the color thought to signify good luck.

Indian Hindu weddings also require the exchange of gifts beforehand and include religious blessings to ensure that the bride and groom have long lives together.

Some indigenous couples in East Malaysia follow other wedding traditions. When a Kadazan couple marries, the bride and groom each place one foot on a stone while someone else places straw hats on their heads. The stone is thought to show how strong the marriage will be, and the hats are meant to protect the bride and groom.

Timeline

People move into the interior of the Malay Peninsula.	**40,000–30,000 years ago**
People begin settling in Borneo.	**ca. 3,000 BCE**
Traders from India reach the Malay Peninsula.	**ca. 100 CE**
Parameswara establishes Melaka.	**ca. 1400**
Islam begins to spread throughout the peninsula.	**ca. 1450**
The Portuguese take control of Melaka.	**1511**
The Dutch and Malay allies take Melaka from the Portuguese.	**1641**
Francis Light brings Penang under the control of the British East India Company.	**1786**
The East India Company creates a colony called the Straits Settlements that includes Melaka, Singapore, and Penang.	**1824**

WORLD HISTORY

ca. 2500 BCE	The Egyptians build the pyramids and the Sphinx in Giza.
ca. 563 BCE	The Buddha is born in India.
313 CE	The Roman emperor Constantine legalizes Christianity.
610	The Prophet Muhammad begins preaching a new religion called Islam.
1054	The Eastern (Orthodox) and Western (Roman Catholic) Churches break apart.
1095	The Crusades begin.
1215	King John seals the Magna Carta.
1300s	The Renaissance begins in Italy.
1347	The plague sweeps through Europe.
1453	Ottoman Turks capture Constantinople, conquering the Byzantine Empire.
1492	Columbus arrives in North America.
1500s	Reformers break away from the Catholic Church, and Protestantism is born.
1776	The U.S. Declaration of Independence is signed.
1789	The French Revolution begins.

MALAYSIAN HISTORY

James Brooke becomes the king of Sarawak.	**1841**
The British government takes control of the Straits Settlements.	**1858**
The British combine four sultanates into the Federated Malay States, with its capital at Kuala Lumpur.	**1896**
Japan takes control of Malaya during World War II.	**1941**
The Federation of Malaya is formed.	**1948**
The Federation of Malaya gains its independence from Great Britain.	**1957**
The nation of Malaysia is formed.	**1963**
Riots between Malays and Chinese follow election results.	**1969**
Mahathir bin Mohamad becomes prime minister and helps modernize Malaysia's economy.	**1981**
Malaysia announces 1Malaysia program to strengthen ethnic unity.	**2010**
One Malaysia Airlines plane disappears and another is shot down.	**2014**

WORLD HISTORY

1865	The American Civil War ends.
1879	The first practical lightbulb is invented.
1914	World War I begins.
1917	The Bolshevik Revolution brings communism to Russia.
1929	A worldwide economic depression begins.
1939	World War II begins.
1945	World War II ends.
1969	Humans land on the Moon.
1975	The Vietnam War ends.
1989	The Berlin Wall is torn down as communism crumbles in Eastern Europe.
1991	The Soviet Union breaks into separate states.
2001	Terrorists attack the World Trade Center in New York City and the Pentagon near Washington, D.C.
2004	A tsunami in the Indian Ocean destroys coastlines in Africa, India, and Southeast Asia.
2008	The United States elects its first African American president.

Fast Facts

Official name: Malaysia

Capital: Kuala Lumpur

Official language: Malay

Kuala Lumpur

National flag

Langkawi Islands

Official religion:	Islam
Year of founding:	1957 for Federation of Malaya, 1963 for Malaysia
National anthem:	"Negaraku" ("My Country")
Type of government:	Constitutional monarchy
Head of state:	King
Head of government:	Prime minister
Area of country:	127,355 square miles (329,848 sq km)
Latitude and longitude of geographic center:	30°2' N, 30°112' E
Bordering countries:	Thailand, Indonesia, Singapore, and Brunei
Highest elevation:	Mount Kinabalu, 13,431 feet (4,094 m) above sea level
Lowest elevation:	Sea level, along the coast
Average high temperature:	In Kuala Lumpur, 90°F (32°C) in January, 91°F (33°C) in July
Average low temperature:	In Kuala Lumpur, 74°F (23°C) in January, 75°F (24°C) in July
Average annual precipitation:	About 150 inches (380 cm) in East Malaysia; 100 inches (250 cm) in West Malaysia

Gunung Mulu National Park

National population (2014 est.):	30.2 million	
Population of major cities (2011 est.):	Kuala Lumpur	1.6 million
	Klang	1.2 million
	Johor Bahru	1 million
	Ipoh	700,000
	Shah Alam	670,000

Landmarks:
- ▶ *Batu Caves*, Kuala Lumpur
- ▶ *Blue Mosque*, Shah Alam
- ▶ *Gunung Mulu National Park*, Sarawak
- ▶ *Petronas Towers*, Kuala Lumpur
- ▶ *Sultan Abdul Samad Building*, Kuala Lumpur

Economy: Malaysia's industry includes the manufacture of semiconductors, computers, and home electronics. Malaysian companies also make chemicals, turn raw rubber and palm oil into finished products, and process agricultural products into food. Malaysian farmers grow many other crops as well, including rice, pepper, coconuts, papayas, and pineapples. The country produces oil and natural gas, most of which is taken from below the sea. Tourism is also an important part of the economy.

Currency

Currency: The ringgit (RM). In 2015, 1 ringgit equaled about US$0.30 and US$1.00 equaled 3.59 ringgit.

System of weights and measures: Metric system

Literacy rate (2010): 97.3%

Schoolchildren

Nicol David

Common Malay words and phrases:

Ya	Yes
Tidak	No
Helo	Hello
Selamat tinggal	Good-bye
Silakan	Please
Terima kasih	Thank you
Sama-sama	You're welcome
Apa kabar?	How are you?
Kabar baik	I'm fine
Nama saya…	My name is…

Prominent Malaysians:

Nicol David (1983–)
Championship squash player

Tony Fernandes (1964–)
Business owner

Redzuawan Ismail (Chef Wan) (1958–)
Chef and author

Mohammad Nor Khalid (Lat) (1951–)
Cartoonist

Parameswara (?–1424)
Founder of Melaka

Tunku Abdul Rahman (1903–1990)
First prime minister

Michelle Yeoh (1962–)
Actor

To Find Out More

Books

▶ Guillain, Charlotte. *Islamic Culture*. Chicago: Heinemann Library, 2013.

▶ Lat. *Kampung Boy*. New York: First Second, 2006.

▶ Owings, Lisa. *Malaysia*. Minneapolis: Bellwether Media, 2014.

▶ Weil, Ann. *Meet Our New Student from Malaysia*. Hockessin, DE: Mitchell Lane Publishers, 2009.

Video

▶ *Discover the World: Malaysia*. KM Records, 2012.

▶ *Travelview International: Malaysia*. CreateSpace, 2009.

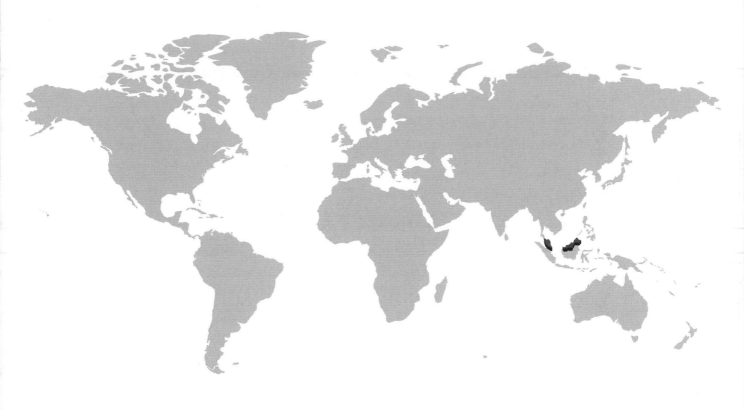

▶ Visit this Scholastic Web site for more information on Malaysia:
www.factsfornow.scholastic.com
Enter the keyword **Malaysia**

Index

Page numbers in *italics* indicate illustrations.

mountains, 16, 18–19, *18*, 22, 24, 96

Peninsular Malaysia, *14*, 15

pinnacles, *22*, *23*

rivers, 16, 19–20, 21, 23

Strait of Malacca, 11, 17–18, *17*

George Town, *50*, 51, 122–123

giant walking sticks, 40, *40*

Gift of Rain, The (Tan Twan Eng), 110

gongs, 108

government

  cabinet, 68

  communications and, 83

  Conference of Rulers, 62

  constitution, 69, 87, 95

  Court of Appeals, 69

  elections, 59, 65, 69

  ethnic groups and, 55, 87

  executive branch, 56–57, *57*, 58, 59, *59*, 61, 63, 66, 67–68, 83, *83*

  Federal Court, 69, *71*

  Federation of Malaya, 55

  Great Britain and, 11–12, 52, 54–55, 61

  High Courts, 69–70

  homestay program, 121

  House of Representatives, 64–65, 67–68

  independence, 55, *55*, 68, 73

  Japanese occupation, 53–54

  judicial branch, 57, 63, 66, 68–70

  kings, *60*, 61, 62, 65–66, 67, 69, 71

  Kuala Lumpur and, 62, 72

  laws, 65, 67, 69, 72

  legislative branch, 62, 64–67, *65*, *67*

  Magistrate Courts, 70

  military, 62

  Ministry of Finance, *72*

  oil industry and, 80

  1Malaysia program, 59, 85

  Parliament, 62, 63, 64–67, *65*, *67*

  police, 64

political parties, 58, *58*, 68

prime ministers, 56–57, *57*, 58, 59, *59*, 61, 67, 68, 83, *83*

religion and, 64, 70, 95, 98

Sekapan people and, 90

Senate, 65–66

Sessions Courts, 70

state governments, 61, 70, 71–72

sultanates, 43, 48, *48*, 50, 51, 52, 54, 61

sultans, 52, 54, 55, 62, 64, 71, 108, 110

taxes, 65

term limits, 65, 66

United Malays National Organisation (UMNO), 58, 68

Unity Squad, 85

women in, 69

Great Britain

  Borneo and, 51

  Brooke family, 51

  East India Company, 50–51, 52

  economy and, 52, 53

  Federated Malay States, 52, 63

  Francis Light, 51, *51*

  government and, 11–12, 52, 54–55, 61

  hill stations and, 19

  Hinduism and, 100

  Islamic religion and, 52

  language and, 93

  Penang Island and, 51

  Residents, 52

  rubber trees and, 29

  Straits Settlements, 51, 52

  sultanates and, 43

  trade and, 50–51

  Unfederated Malay States, 52

gross domestic product (GDP), 76

guay cakes, 123

Gunung Mulu National Park, *22*, 23

H

Hang Tuah, 108

Harmony Silk Factory, The (Tash Aw), 109–110

hawksbill sea turtles, 36

health care, 68, 81

High Courts, 69–70

hijab (clothing), 122

hill stations, 19

Hinduism, 45, 89, 95, 99–100, *99*, *100*, 101, 103, 127

historical maps. *See also* maps.

  British Territories in Southeast Asia (1940), 53

  Melaka Sultanate (1500), 48

  Straits Settlements (1900), *52*

  Trade Routes in Southeast Asia (12th Century), *46*

Hokkien language, 90

holidays

  national, *64*, 103, 126, *126*

  religious, 103

homestay program, 121

House of Representatives, 64–65, 67–68

housing, 9, 25, 50, 78, 112, 120–121, *121*

hydroelectricity, 21

I

Iban people, 45, 88, 107

Ibrahim Hussein, 111, *111*

immigration, 12, 45, 63

independence, 55, *55*, 64, 68, 73

Independence Day, 64

Indian people, 12, 45–46, 53, 54–55, 89, *89*, 99, 127

indigenous people, *39*, 44–45, 62, 70, 87–88, 95–96, *96*, 105, 127

Indonesia, 16, 17, *17*, 31, 46, 76, 77, 90, 108, 113

insect life, 34, 40–41, *40*, *41*

International Space Station, 98
Internet, 83
Ipoh, 20, *20*, 79, 86
irrigation, 22
Iskandar Shah (prince), 47
Islamic Arts Museum, 110, *110*
Islamic religion, 20, 43, 47, 52, 64,
    69, 70, 87, *94*, 95, 97–99, *97*, 103,
    110, 113, 118, 122, 124
islands. *See also* Borneo.
    Banggi, 15
    Langkawi, *14*, 15
    number of, 15, 16
    Penang, 15, 51
Iron Lasah, 90

J

Jakun people, 45
Jamek Mosque, 63
Japan, 53–54, 75
jawi alphabet, 93, *93*
Johor, 20, 48, *100*, 115, *123*
Johor Bahru, 20, *20*, 86
Judaism, 97–98
judicial branch of government, 57,
    63, 66, 68–70

K

Kadazan people, 45, 88, 122
Kampung Boy (Lat), 112
Kee Thuan Chye, 110
kenduri (celebration feasts), 126
kerises (curved knives), 108, *108*
Kinabatangan River, 16, 23
king cobras, 35, *35*
kings, *60*, 61, 62, 65–66, 67, 69,
    71
Kinta River, 20
kite flying, 115, *115*
Klang, 20, 86
Kuala Lumpur. *See also* cities.
    airport, 82

architecture in, 10, *11*, 63
Chinatown, *56*
Christianity in, *102*
climate, 16
families in, 117
Federated Malay States and, 63
government and, 62, 72
Islamic Arts Museum, 110, *110*
Kuala Lumpur Railway Station, 63
map of, *63*
marketplaces in, *84*, *104*
mosques, *94*
Parliament in, 63, 65
Petronas Towers, 10, *11*, 63
population, 20, 63, 86
service industries in, 81
soccer in, *115*
Sultan Abdul Samad Building,
    63, *63*
temples in, *12*

L

Labuan, 62, 72
Langkawi Islands, *14*, 15
languages, 12, 73, 82–83, 87, 89,
    90–93, *92*, 98, 109
Lat, 112, 133
Latiff Mohidin, 111
laws, 65, 67, 69, 72
leatherback sea turtles, 36
Lee Chong Wei, 114
legislative branch of government, 62,
    64–67, *65*, *67*
Legoland Resort Malaysia, 20
Light, Francis, 51, *51*
lionfish, 37, *37*
literacy rate, 86
literature, 109–110, *110*
livestock, 77
lobsters, 78, *78*
longhouses, 121, *121*

M

Magistrate Courts, 70
Mahathir bin Mohamad, 56–57, *57*
Mah Meri people, *96*
mak yong (dance-drama), 8
Malay Annals, 47
Malayan tapirs, 32, *32*, 33
Malayan tigers (national animal), 28,
    30, *30*, 33
Malay Archipelago, 15
Malay language, 47, 73, 85, 87, 90,
    92–93, *92*, 98, 109
Malay Peninsula, 9, 17
Malaysiakini newspaper, 83
Malaysian Airlines, 59, *59*
manufacturing, *74*, 80–81
maps. *See also* historical maps.
    geopolitical, *10*
    Kuala Lumpur, *63*
    Malaysian States and Federal
        Territories, *62*
    population density, *86*
    resources, *77*
    topographical, *16*
marine life, 36–37, *37*, 77, 78, *78*
marketplaces, *84*, *104*
marriage, 69, 108, 127, *127*
masks, 107, *107*
Mecca, Saudi Arabia, 98
Melaka, 46, 47, *47*, 48–49, *48*, 51, 89,
    107, 120, 133
metalworking, 108, *108*
migrant workers, 90, *91*
military, 62
Minangkabau people, 112
mining, 52, 79, *79*, 80
Ministry of Finance, *72*
Mohammad Nor Khalid, 112, 133
monarchs, *60*, 61, 62, 65–66, 67, 69, 71
monitor lizards, 36
monsoons, 24
mosques, 20, 63, *94*, 95, 97, *97*, 112

Federated Malay States, 52, 63
governments of, 61, 70, 71–72
Johor, 20, 48, *100*, 115, *123*
map of, *53*
Melaka, 46, 47, *47*, 48–49, *48*, 51,
    89, *107*, 120, 133
Penang, 13, *24*, 52, *74*, 90, 120,
    122
Perak, 20, 73
Sabah, 22, 23, 55, 62, 70, 77, 78,
    87, 88, 107, 108, 117, 122
Sarawak, 22, 23, *42*, 51, 55, 62,
    70, 77, 86, 88, 96, 107, *119*,
    121, 122
Selangor, 20, 86
Unfederated Malay States, 52
Strait of Johor, 20
Strait of Malacca, 11, 17–18, *17*
Straits Settlements, 51, 52
street food, *124*
Sulawesi, 49–50
Sultan Abdul Samad Building, 63, *63*
sultanates, 43, 48, *48*, 50, 51, 52, 54,
    61
sultans, 52, 54, 55, 62, 64, 71, 108,
    110
Sumatra, 11, 17, *17*, 31, 46, 47
Sumatran rhinoceroses, 30, 33
swiftlets, 38, *38*
syariah courts, 70

T
Taman Negara National Park, 18–19,
    33
Tamil Nadu (India), 89
Tamil people, 89, 100
Tan Aik Huang, 114
Tan Twan Eng, 109, *110*
Tash Aw, 109–110
tattooing, 90, 108
taxes, 65
teak trees, 28

technology industries, *74*, 80, 81, *81*
television, 83, 110
tempeh, 124
Temple Cave, 100
textile industry, *104*, 106–107, *106*
Thailand, 15
timber industry, 28, *28*, 78
tin industry, 20, 52, 79, *79*
Tin Museum, 20
Titiwangsa Mountains, 18, *18*
tops, 120, *120*
tourism, 13, *13*, *18*, 36, 81, 121
towns. *See also* cities; villages.
    flooding in, 25, *25*
    governments in, 72
    hill stations as, 19
    population of, 86
    transportation in, 82
trade, 10–11, 45, 46, 48, 50–51, 54, 75
transportation, 17–18, *49*, 59, *59*, 82,
    83
tualang plants, 28
Tunku Abdul Rahman, 68, *68*, 83,
    83, 133
typhoons, 24–25

U
Unfederated Malay States, 52
United Malays National Organisation
    (UMNO), 58, 68
United States, 53, 70, 75, 123
Unity Squad, 85

V
villages. *See also* cities; towns.
    children in, *87*, 90
    clothing in, 122
    Kampung Boy (Lat) and, 112
    housing in, 120–121, *121*
    metalworking in, 108
    population of, 86, 90
    religion in, 95, 108

W
waterbirds, 39
wau bulan kites, 115, *115*
West Malaysia, 15–16, 17–19, 21, 28,
    33, 86
wildflowers, 27, 30, *30*
wildlife. *See* amphibian life; animal
    life; insect life; marine life; plant
    life; reptilian life.
women, 69, *69*, 99, 113, 117, 121, 122
World War II, 53–54, *54*

Y
Yeoh, Michelle, 112–113, 133
Yuna, 113, *113*

Z
Zainah Anwar, 69, *69*
Zang Toi, 113

Meet the Author

MICHAEL BURGAN IS INTRIGUED BY PLACES where different cultures mixed, including Malaysia. Since he did not have a chance to travel to Malaysia to research this book, he relied on the expertise of others. He turned to books and Web sites and interviewed Johari Abdullah, who spent his childhood in Malaysia.

This is Burgan's fifth book in the Enchantment of the World series. Previously, he wrote about Belgium, Chile, Kenya, and the United States. Over his career, Burgan has written more than 250 books for children and teens, most them about history or geography. Some of his other books for Children's Press include *The U.S. Constitution* and *American Capitalism*.

Burgan graduated from the University of Connecticut with a degree in history. In his free time, he writes plays and enjoys traveling and taking pictures. He also edits the newsletter for Biographers International Organization (BIO). Burgan lives in Santa Fe, New Mexico, with his cat, Callie.

Photo Credits

Peachtree

Atlanta-Fulton Public Library

10/15